Integration Alchemy

The Real Ceremony Is Your Life

Praise for *Integration Alchemy*

"Psychedelic experiences open doors, but integration is what allows us to truly live in the new rooms. In *Integration Alchemy*, Deva Arani offers a heartfelt and sophisticated roadmap for this essential part of the journey. Bridging the scientific and the sacred, she reminds us that the real ceremony begins when the medicine fades and consciousness becomes daily practice."

—**Rick Doblin, Ph.D.,** Founder and President, Multidisciplinary Association for Psychedelic Studies (MAPS)

"With humility, precision, and warmth, Deva Arani invites us into the living work of integration, where the insights of ceremony become pathways of embodied change. Rooted in trauma-informed sensitivity and a deep reverence for the sacred, this book honors both the vulnerability and the courage required to truly heal. It is a trustworthy companion for anyone walking the tender bridge between revelation and real life."

—**Matt Licata, PhD**, author of *A Healing Space: Befriending Ourselves in Difficult Times*

"In *Integration Alchemy*, Deva gently guides the reader with a steady, loving hand through the inner and outer journey of integration. Her lived experience, embodied practices and accumulated wisdom are a valuable resource for anyone, both before and after plant medicine ceremony."

—**Sat Dharam Kaur ND**

"*Integration Alchemy* by Deva Arani is a thoughtful and much-needed reflection on the 'psychedelic renaissance,' a movement whose antinomianism sits uneasily alongside the spiritual traditions of humanity and their sacred epistemologies. Given the current mntal health epidemic, and its roots in today's spiritual crisis, many are looking to entheogens for relief. However, these are not a panacea. A key question that arises when assessing this phenomenon is: How can people access these sacred medicines in a safe and discerning manner? Arani intimately explores her time spent with spiritual guides in both the Andes and the Amazon basin of South America. She offers seekers various ways in which to think about the use of traditional remedies in support of our journey toward healing and wholeness."

—**Samuel Bendeck Sotillos, PsyD, LPCC, LMFT,** author of *Psyche and the Sacred: Integrating Mental Health and Spiritual Well-Being*

"There is so much to say about integration after deep work in expanded states that even a week-long workshop devoted entirely to integrative practices can feel incomplete. Arani's book is comprehensive, touching every aspect of the process. It is relevant not only to participants in medicine ceremonies but also to those who practice Holotropic Breathwork (one of my own modalities of choice) or engage in any form of deep inner work. Her writing is clear, concise, and kind. Through generous stories from her own experience, Arani offers invaluable insight into working with entheogens while guiding readers through the nuances of integrative practice. Body, mind, and spirit are all addressed with equal depth and care. I myself have received steady, grounded support from Arani over the years. By reading this book, you will join me in that receiving. It is a true gift."

—**Sharanya Naik,** Facilitator and Practitioner of Holotropic Breathwork™

"Deva Arani is deeply committed to her work with plant medicine, meditation practice, and therapeutic training. She has woven these paths into her daily life with sincerity and devotion. She now brings her knowledge, experience, and love to support others. She has been a steady source of inspiration and encouragement for me, and this book gathers her wisdom into an extraordinary resource for those walking a path of healing."

—**Nanda Nina Lynch,** Rinzai Zen Priest

"*Integration Alchemy* is a much-needed guide for anyone who has opened to something profound in ceremony and wondered how to bring that awakening back into daily life. Deva Arani writes with both reverence for the lineages she carries and a deep, lived understanding of the nervous system, embodiment, and true integration. This book is a grounded companion for the long, spiraling journey of genuine transformation."

—**Jennifer McKeever, RCC, CCC,** Somatic Psychotherapist, Breathwork Teacher, and Path of Love Leader

"*Integration Alchemy* offers a grounded, trauma-informed framework for transforming expanded-state experiences into lasting psychological and relational growth. With precision, compassion, and deep skill, Deva Arani illuminates the essential practices that support true and sustainable integration. This is a valuable resource for clinicians and seekers alike."

—**Nirodha Stearns, MA LPCC**

"I have witnessed Deva Arani's clarity, integrity, and unwavering devotion to the healing path for years. With *Integration Alchemy*, she brings together her hard-earned wisdom in a guide that is at once practical, accessible, and profoundly illuminating. It embodies the same grounded presence she offers in her work—real support for the lifelong journey of transformation."

—**Nooraya Sophia Wales,** Transformational Coach, Breathwork facilitator, and Visual Artist

"*Integration Alchemy* is a rare and essential guide for anyone seeking to understand the deeper meaning of their psychedelic or ceremonial experiences. Drawing from decades of lived practice, Deva Arani offers a grounded, soulful, and deeply compassionate approach to integrating expanded states into the fabric of daily life. Her writing illuminates the subtle terrain between insight and embodiment, inviting readers to walk the path of healing with clarity and integrity. This book will be a trusted companion to journeyers from many traditions, supporting them long after the ceremony ends."

—**Scott Lines, Ph.D.,** Licensed Clinical Psychologist and Certified Psychedelic Therapist

Integration Alchemy

The Real Ceremony Is Your Life

Deva Arani

First Sentient Publications edition year 2026

A paperback original

Book design by Laura Johanna Waltje
Cover Art by Juca Maximo
Cover Design by Laura Johanna Waltje
Illustrations by Fatima Seehar

Library of Congress Control Number: 2025941561
Publisher's Cataloging-in-Publication Data
Names: Shimer Tanya R., author.
Title: Integration alchemy : the real ceremony is your life / Deva Arani.
Description: Boulder, CO: Sentient Publications, 2026.
Identifiers: LCCN: 2025941561 | ISBN: 978-1-59181-367-5 (paperback) | 978-1-59181-368-2 (epub)
Subjects: LCSH Hallucinogenic drugs--Therapeutic use. | Psychopharmacology. | Altered states of consciousness. | Alternative medicine. | Spiritual life. | BISAC BODY, MIND & SPIRIT / Entheogens & Visionary Substances | SELF-HELP / Spiritual | BODY, MIND & SPIRIT / Inspiration & Personal Growth
Classification: LCC RM324.8 .A73 2026 | DDC 615.7883--dc23

SENTIENT PUBLICATIONS
A Limited Liability Company
PO Box 1851
Boulder, CO 80306
www.sentientpublications.com

For the sacred medicines
and the teachers who carry their songs.

Contents

Part Three:
Our Ceremony Unfolds

Acknowledgment

I offer this work in honor of those who walked before me—the wisdom keepers, the medicine carriers, the ones who remembered the sacred in all things. I bow to the ancestors who lived in harmony with the land, who sang to the waters and prayed with their feet pressed into the soil. I honor the Indigenous stewards of sacred plants and ceremonies, whose traditions continue to guide healing across generations. This work would not exist without them. It belongs to the great web of life, and to those who hold it with humility, respect, and care.

I honor my own ancestors: those who knew how to love fully and lived in right relationship with nature, with spirit, and with one another. I also remember those who forgot the sacred ceremony of life, who passed on pain because they lost the path to peace in their own beings. I hold them in compassion. I remember what they forgot: that healing, no matter how delayed, is still possible and that life itself is the ceremony.

To all who came before, I bow. May this book be a bridge between worlds, between timelines, between the broken and the whole. May it serve not only my healing, but the healing of the collective body to which we all belong.

My love and gratitude extend to Swami Anand Samir and Buddha dog Ben. Together, we have shared the light of love and the silent truth of the ceremony that exists in every breath, every moment, here and now.

I thank my teachers and acknowledge that this book comes through me, but it is from them—their lives, their wisdom, and their love. This medicine is not mine to claim. It belongs to them, and I pray that it is worthy of their grace. I am forever grateful for their presence and for their guidance on this long journey home to myself.

My deepest gratitude to my editor extraordinaire, Emily Graf whose idea it was for me to revisit this book on integration and encouraged me to do so with her kind heart and wisdom; and to my publisher, Sentient Publications and Steven Harrison, who kindly met with me to discuss this project, and when I asked which book I should write (as prior to this our conversations had been about my next book), he simply replied, "Well, obviously both." Their trust in my finding my voice in this important dialogue about integration is what has made this book possible.

Author's Preface

"Live your life like it's a banner written on the sky."

This was my beloved Samir's advice to me many years ago. He shared these words long before I realized that he was the love of my life, and my most precious fellow traveler on the sacred journey home to myself. I was entering my first residential group intensive, a very intimidating journey to self, called the Path of Love. This group was my first deep dive into claiming my real and authentic self, in a visible way. This was many years before I met the sacred plant medicines discussed in this book, and I admit humbly that it has taken me twenty plus years to finally truly embrace Samir's wisdom and embody it.

Indeed, this is my second attempt to write a book on the integration of entheogens and specifically my experience integrating sacred plant medicines. For many years before my first attempt, I had quietly been supporting people one-on-one, by word of mouth, as they tried to make sense of the profound experiences they had during ceremonies. Repeatedly, I saw that integration was where people struggled. Many tried to chase the light they'd touched by seeking more medicine, more ceremony, more peak experiences—without being given the tools to root that insight into their daily lives. I felt called to offer something that could help.

So, I set out to write a book.

I hired a book coach who came highly recommended, trusting that structured support would help me bring my vision to life. At the time, I was eager to complete the project and welcomed her framework. Looking back, I can see that in following her prescribed process—writing chapters quickly as assignments—I prioritized finishing over deep reflection and revision. The result was a book that successfully conveyed the importance of integration, yet it didn't fully capture the depth or voice I now recognize as essential to this work.

I had made a significant investment, both financially and emotionally, and the experience became a profound teacher. When I was later invited to join the coach's next publishing program for an additional cost, I realized that I wanted to take full ownership of my creative process. I chose to publish the book independently, and Integration Alchemy: Rekindle Your Transformational Retreat and Shine was released on Amazon in July 2019. It reached the people it needed to reach, and their encouragement reminded me that the journey of writing, like integration itself, is one of continual learning and refinement.

But here's the truth: it wasn't my voice.

At that time, I wasn't ready to publicly acknowledge my relationship with entheogens. I cloaked the language in transformational retreat vocabulary and wrote from the persona of a life coach. I even chose a painting of Green Tara for the cover that looked psychedelic and explained to my friends that it was my code. It felt like a disguise. That book was a compromise. Embarrassing? Yes. Public? Also, yes. But it was a necessary step.

After a few months, I pulled the book from Amazon. Every time I thought about rewriting it, I felt a sharp pain in my chest. I had to sit with the vulnerability of being seen, offering what had once been my private journey with plant medicine to others with an open heart. To write the book I was meant to write, I had to come out. Not just as an author, but as someone deeply connected to sacred plant medicine traditions, even if that meant being misunderstood by my Christian family or others in my life. Even though I worked in Peru where sacred plant medicine is legal, as an attorney I worried about being seen in this light.

Six years later, I was invited by my publisher to write the book I had always meant to write. A real book. A true book. One that emerges from my lived experience, my real voice, and my reverence for the sacred plant medicine lineages of South America. I said yes.

In the years between the first book and this one, I deepened my own integration and understanding of how healing happens outside of ceremony. I completed the year-long Compassionate Inquiry® professional training, a deeply trauma-informed, relational approach that integrates body-based awareness with attuned, compassionate exploration. These foundations continue to inform how I support others. This learning not only transformed my sessions, but it also gave me language and structure for the healing I had always sensed was possible and had experienced myself, through more esoteric modalities, group processes, and meditation practices.

There are moments in sacred medicine work when a buried truth rises to the surface, illuminated by the intelligence of the plants. What was once hidden in the body—an old grief, an unmet need, a forgotten tenderness—suddenly becomes clear and alive. The medicine often shows us scenes from the past, not as memories to analyze, but as living sensations that can finally be felt and released. These visions are the language of the body speaking in images, revealing where energy has been frozen in time. Healing does not happen through the mind's understanding alone; it unfolds through presence, breath, and the willingness to feel what was once unbearable. Medicine can open the door, but integration is what allows the body to complete what it could not before. True transformation takes place as we bring this awareness into the small gestures of daily life—through gentleness, relationship, and the slow, ongoing return to embodied wholeness.

Over the last several decades, I have walked a path that integrates Eastern traditions of meditation and yoga with the sacred plant lineages of the Amazon and Andes. I've sat in *dieta* with grandmother ayahuasca, walked with grandfather huachuma, and listened to the whisper of ancient wisdom through jungle, desert, mountain, and ocean. And while my path has been long, I see today that many are coming to the medicine younger, faster, and more urgently. The quickening is real. Our world is more fragmented, more uncertain than ever, and the medicine is responding.

But with that quickening comes responsibility.

It is not enough to experience transformation in ceremony. We must anchor it into our lives. That is the purpose of this book. Integration is not something we check off a list. It is a living practice: a return to the body, to presence, to trust, to love. It is how our lives become the ceremony.

This book is an offering. I offer it in reciprocity for all that I have received on my own path, including the many remarkable teachers who have shared their wisdom and medicine with me over all these years. Words cannot express my gratitude for their help and support in shining a light for me to follow. May this book shine a light for you to support you in remembering who you are, why you came here, and how to walk in a good way with what has been revealed.

"The plants have been our teachers since the beginning. They do not speak in our language, but if we learn to listen, they will show us the way back to ourselves."

– Unknown

Introduction:

Integration And the Ceremony of Life

"The privilege of a lifetime is to become who you really are."
—Carl Jung

When we experience sacred plant medicine, we are given a glimpse of a higher possibility within our beings. Attending a plant medicine ceremony is a privilege that few people on this earth experience. If you can grasp the sacred miracle that these plants are and understand that your experience with them was not accidental, but rather an intrinsic part of the divine order of existence, you can then realize that your life is connected to something beyond this three-dimensional realm we humans inhabit. The sacred plant's vibration is an invitation for your life that can be carried forward into the ordinary reality that makes up our world. Life is precious and meaningful; to embody this, sometimes we must realign our trajectory.

In this book, I invite you on an inner journey of exploration. This book is an invitation to explore the interwoven threads of the human experience and thus access the subtle plane which exists within each of us. Integration can be approached by first gently examining the different aspects of the human experience—including the body, mind, and emotions—as distinct, each with its own needs, wounds, and wisdom. By exploring and honoring these parts separately, we gain clarity and compassion for how they function and interact. Integration then becomes the conscious act of weaving these aspects back together through understanding and awareness—creating the possibility of a more integrated, whole being in service of authenticity.

If you are reading this book, you most likely have journeyed with a sacred plant medicine or are contemplating undertaking such a journey. You might have had experiences with psychedelics in the past and are now seeking deeper intentionality in your work, perhaps healing or spiritual understanding. You might have participated in many journeys with plant medicines and are finding that repetition to feel the peak experience over and over is starting to feel counterproductive. Whether you are entering the stream for the first time, exiting the stream for the first time, or trying to make more out of many trips down river: if you've picked up this book, you are probably seeking to better understand and embody your experience. If you bought this book as a part of your preparation journey, this book will be very helpful to you as well, and I have also provided some specific suggestions for preparation in Appendix One.

One way to approach this book is to work with it as a ceremony. Our ceremony guests include all of our intelligence centers—including body, mind, and emotions—that need attention and care during integration. Each participant has come to be healed and understood in the ceremony that is your life. You are the shaman of this ceremony. Treat each participant as you would a treasured companion who has come to you for healing. Think of each center as equally important guests in your ceremony to tend to with loving care and curiosity; offer attention, support and kindness.

"We do not use the medicine; the medicine uses us if we are open, if we listen."

—Peruvian Healer

My journey with sacred plant medicine has truly been an unfolding. It was never my intention to work with Indigenous healers and sacred plant medicines. In fact, these medicines weren't even on my radar for many years, as I thought my spiritual healing journey was based solely on the Eastern traditions of meditation and yoga. However, the medicine had a different idea and before I knew it, I found myself in the Amazon Rainforest on my first sacred plant *dieta*. A dieta is a traditional plant diet and usually spans two weeks in isolation in the jungle working with the *plantas maestras* (master plant teachers) including ayahuasca. What a surprise, what a gift, what a benediction for my life in this body. Over the past twenty years or so I have had the privilege of spending considerable time in the rainforests of the Amazon and Andes of Peru working with Indigenous wisdom keepers and healers there, many of whom are now my chosen family. I have been on numerous (I stopped counting at twenty-plus) sacred plant dietas, and I feel so humble, and I am so grateful that I was invited to do this work in this lifetime with such impeccable and integral teachers. To these teachers, I offer a deep bow. The sacred plantas maestros and maestras that I have met and worked with on my many dietas are allies that I treasure and nurture within my very being. I share my perspectives on integration from this place of experience, for each time I return home to the States from down South I have to piece myself back together and show up in this life that I lead here, now.

While my experience that I am sharing in this book is centered on working in South America with the entheogens that originate there, such as grandmother ayahuasca, grandfather huachuma, chirac sanango, and others; this book is meant for all friends on the spiritual path who are experiencing and exploring entheogen experiences. By entheogen, I mean all the remarkable *consciousness altering* plants and medicines,[1] as well as any intense process, such as group intensive work like The Path of Love group process, Holotropic Breathwork, etc., that brings you to a place of *needing to integrate* because the experience changed or challenged your normal point of reference in life. For the sake of simplicity, throughout this book I refer to all these various experiences as sacred plant medicine experiences or journeys, because any time we dive deep enough to get beyond the veil of the three-dimensional realm, we become connected to sacred medicine.

---

1 Commonly recognized entheogens include traditional plant medicines that have been in relation with us humans for millennia: Ayahuasca, Psilocybin Mushrooms, Peyote, San Pedro (Huachuma), Iboga, Bufo alvarius (5-MeO-DMT), Kambo, Cannabis, Syrian Rue, Salvia Divinorum, and Amanita muscaria; as well more modern "man made" discoveries: LSD, MDMA, DMT (synthetic), Ketamine, and Mescaline (synthetic).

Integration And the Ceremony of Life

I was taught that in the Indigenous traditions of the Amazon, in ancient times, the *curandero* (shaman) would prepare the sacred medicine and people who were called to participate would find their way to the ceremony, sometimes walking for days or weeks through the jungle in solitary pilgrimage, following an inner directive to arrive at the sacred circle which would then unfold after everyone invited had arrived. Each participant was a meaningful and intrinsic part of the whole. It is my understanding that this unfolding and invitation from the plantas maestras continues with our participation today.

Since I started my journey with the sacred plant medicines, I have witnessed an explosion of interest in this area. As more and more opportunities become available for Westerners to partake, I feel it becomes more important to emphasize that these medicinal experiences are not separate from your life and can offer a guidepost for continued growth, expansion, and maturity, with integration. During this time of global instability, the sacred plants are purposefully spreading their light, intentionally expanding beyond their traditional landscapes to help us remember and reconnect with that which we have forgotten: Mother Earth, Father Sun, the Sacred, the Divine.

Westerners who experience plant medicine ceremonies almost always feel a sense of wonder and awe—an openness and connectedness that is both healing and familiar—and often disconcerting and disorienting afterwards. If you are reading this book, it probably means that you've been on a journey that affected your physical, mental and emotional bodies, your sense of perception, and your state of consciousness.

While one can experience difficulties during ceremony, the real challenge is in landing at home—and finding ourselves in what might feel like a foreign land—our day-to-day life. As a seeker, you experienced a possibility beyond your ordinary state of consciousness that stoked a longing. Now you are home, and your world is not the same, because *you* are not the same. Something inside you was touched, inspired, *rekindled,* and you are struggling to integrate it into your real life: your routines, your relationships, your work, and the way you move in the world.

Now that you are home, you might feel as if the people in your life—even the people you are closest to—are not receptive to your experience. You might have tried to share your experience of ceremony: what you felt, experienced, and received, only to see your friends or family respond with skepticism or indifference. In relating, you might miss the deep connection and acceptance you felt with your fellow travelers who shared the ceremony with you.

As you move through your days, your responsibilities and activities might feel like more of a burden than ever before, and you might be wondering why you can't gain traction in making the changes you had committed to during your journey.

On your journey, you might have felt your heart to be open and full of love in a way that you didn't think was possible before. You might have felt a deep connection with your fellow travelers, accepted and loved for just being you, and now you feel the lack of this authentic connection with the people in your life. You might also have felt a connection and a oneness with nature and the divine and hoped that this sense of wonder and grace would never leave you.

You might also have worked to heal some wounds from your childhood and uncovered how they are impacting your life here and now. In the ceremony, you were able to see beneath the surface that you have not yet fully addressed some of the unconscious patterns that you developed to survive a childhood in this body, this human form. You might be in considerable pain or feeling the weight of some trauma you uncovered and wondering how it will ever be fully healed and transformed into grace, because now it just feels muddy, sticky, and too much.

You had an experience: maybe you felt your heart fully for the first time; maybe you were able to see and work on healing deep wounds from childhood trauma; maybe you felt a deep and enriching connection to your fellow travelers, nature, and the divine. You might have gained insight into the choices you have made and where you find yourself as a result. Maybe you opened up and made a commitment to your spiritual self or the divine; maybe you landed in a space of deep gratitude. These alchemical experiences made you aware of some part of you that you either lost or forgot, a remembrance or experience of a higher possibility within you. Without integration, the medicine's message is scattered on the wind, and we are drawn once again into our old stories, adaptive patterns, and habits.

To truly integrate and embody our experience, we have to put forth intention and effort. The real ceremony takes place in our day-to-day world when our lives reflect the generosity, wisdom, love and compassion that the sacred plant medicines share with us. Receiving the miracle of the medicine is a gift. If you can think of it as a journey of a thousand lifetimes to be invited to partake, perhaps that framing can encourage, support and nourish your integration journey. Integration is a journey: a journey back to you and your true self. This book is an invitation for you to embark on this journey with support and guidance. The journey is arduous and at times it might feel like one step forward and two steps back, but the truth is your integration journey itself is the destination. The real ceremony is your life.

What Is Integration and Why Does It Matter?

When we work with plant medicine, we have experiences that take us beyond our ordinary state of consciousness. We embark on a journey that can take us through time and space in ways that seem other worldly and yet surprisingly also familiar. Our state of consciousness expands for a period, and then it contracts back to our ordinary state of being and awareness. In essence, we travel beyond our three-dimensional world into a world that exists beyond the three-dimensional veil that contains our reality.

What we experience and receive during that time of expanded consciousness is as myriad and unique as each of us are as individuals. For the purposes of this book, integration is the bringing of what we received in that expanded state into our ordinary consciousness so that we can then fully metabolize it and embody it. When we can harmonize with and embody our experience it brings us closer to wholeness. Integration thus can be understood as an alchemical process of embodiment, where our experience, the insights, and understanding received, are translated into a pathway to wholeness.

Each time we have an opportunity to heal or learn about ourselves we become more whole. Altering or expanding our state of consciousness can be a *dis*integration of our patterns and identifications: the process of breaking into pieces. We can think of integration as bringing those pieces back together into a new and more harmonious whole.

One of the keys to integration is the understanding that we start out whole and that our journey of integration is a returning, a remembering, a recentering into that wholeness that has and will always be who we are, despite all the layers that we have accumulated while being human in this world. In this book we will spend some time understanding wholeness and what keeps us from experiencing and embodying our wholeness to support your integration process.

Integration is an Inner Journey

"A real ceremony is never over. It continues to live inside the people who were touched by it, and it unfolds its teaching over many moons."
—Martín Prechtel

The journey of integration is an inner one and is usually accompanied by a longing to feel more whole. Feeling whole is rooted in two internal experiences: a sense of self-connection and a sense of being centered. Being centered means living and responding from your innermost self, rather than reacting to outer circumstances. It is a grounded presence rooted in your innate wisdom, rather than in accumulated knowledge or external influence.

When we feel connected and centered, we are rooted in our beings. When we are rooted in our beings, we are then able to expand and deepen on all levels. Connection and centeredness are embodied; these qualities are not thoughts coming from the mind or emotions coming from the heart, but rather a felt sense that is both internal and eternal. Our integration quest is an invitation, a remembrance, a homecoming.

Picture a large gong. Imagine the soundwaves of this gong resonating, the healing frequency rippling outward, the vibration continuing long after the mallet hits the metal. Now imagine someone putting their hand on the gong. The vibration stops abruptly. By intentionally seeking to work and show up to honor your ceremony experience, you are allowing the vibration to continue, to resonate in your being. This book is an invitation to allow that vibration to continue to resonate in your life, your true ceremony.

Though I share particularly in terms of the plant medicines of South America ayahuasca and hauchuma, the information in this book will be useful for travelers integrating any type of sacred plant medicine ceremony, peak experience, or healing event.

In this book I hope to help you to alchemize your plant medicine experience, to help you embody the healing and understanding that you received.

To do so is to then become aware that your life is a sacred ceremony designed specifically for you in this body—to heal and learn, to teach and to return.

I have been blessed with many opportunities to heal and become more whole, and I want to honor the work that I have done thus far by inviting this unity to manifest in my ordinary day-to-day world, to walk in my life as ceremony. Part of this walk is reciprocity, and so I offer this book as such and give thanks to the teachers in my life who have generously shone a light for me to follow and gently guided me along my way.

"This place where you are right now, God circled on a map for you.
Wherever your eyes and arms and heart can move Against the earth and the sky,
The Beloved has bowed there –Our beloved has bowed there knowing you were coming."

—Hafiz

This book is structured in three parts following the arc of a traditional sacred ceremony as a metaphor for the integration journey. Part Onc: "Creating a Safe Container for Integration" lays the groundwork for healing through grounding, intention, boundaries, and inner preparation, just as a ceremonial space must be held with safety and reverence. Part Two: "Welcoming Our Guests to Our Ceremony" explores the essential aspects of our inner world that often arise after ceremony: the energy centers of the navel, mind, and emotional body. These are the parts of ourselves, longing to be seen, heard, and healed, that appear like honored guests in need of our attention. Part Three: "Our Ceremony Unfolds" brings the journey full circle by exploring how healing unfolds over time. Here, we enter the true work of integration: practicing attunement, embodying change, and allowing our lives to become the ceremony.

Part 1
Creating a Safe Container for Integration

"Our elders say that ceremonies are the way we can remember to remember."

—Robin Wall Kimmerer

Just as a sacred ceremony begins with the creation of a safe container, where all who enter can be held, protected, and supported, so too does the work of integration. Before we can weave insights into our lives, we must tend the ground that will hold them. This means rooting ourselves in presence—becoming aware of the ways we resist what arises—and honoring the truth that healing is never a straight line, but a spiral. In this first part, we lay the foundation, a container strong enough to hold our process, yet spacious enough to allow the unfolding to move in its own rhythm and time.

Chapter One:

Ceremony, A Living Vibration

When we partake in sacred plant ceremonies, we enter a container for healing and self-knowledge. These Indigenous ceremonies, no matter their tribal origin, are typically comprised of rituals and rhythm. In the ayahuasca tradition from South America that I am blessed to be a part of, we sit in a circle inside a round *maloca*, the traditional ceremony temple. We begin with the ritual of calling in the medicine and setting the intention for our ceremony—*cura cura cuerpicito, limpia limpia almacita*[2]. We then honor the Four Directions by bowing to each and blowing camphor, asking for protection and inviting these energies to attend, and to set our container.

After serving the medicine we invite a period of silence to allow the medicine's presence to be felt. Then the work of healing begins and is supported with the vibration of the shaman's *icaros* (healing songs much like mantras), his rattle and his drum. He might go around the circle and offer individual healings and blessings, known as *limpias*, as well. As the ceremony goes on the intensity of the sacred icaros is balanced with the soothing music of the *charango*, flute, guitar, and periods of rest and silence. At some point toward the end of the ceremony, friends are invited to participate by offering their own music and songs, and finally we close the ceremony with another sacred ritual expressing gratitude and releasing the spirits back to their realms, once again bowing to the Four Directions.

---

2 Heal the body, clean the soul.

The energy of the ceremony manifests as a healing vibration that invites presence in a supported space. The space allows for real sensitivity, real feeling, and real awakening to occur within a safe and protected field. These characteristics of healing, presence, and awakening with sensitivity to the more subtle vibrations of existence also reside within our beings. When we honor this reality, we can approach our life as a sacred ceremony and it becomes such. Integration is the journey to realize our life as ceremony: here, now. Sacred plant medicine journeys have a rhythm, and if you can be aware of this rhythm as an ongoing process, the rhythm can support your integration.

The rhythm of the ceremony unfolds in a sacred space, often a round maloca, where participants are held and supported by the shaman in the safety of a circle.

Symbols Of Wholeness: Circles and Serpents

"The whole world is a circle. All of these circular images reflect the psyche."

—Joseph Campbell

In both the Amazonian and Andean medicine traditions I am blessed to be a part of, the serpent is a revered teacher: a symbol of transformation, deep wisdom, and the spiral of life itself. In the Amazon, the Great Anaconda, known as *Yacumama*, is seen as the spirit of the jungle: a primordial force that connects water, earth, and memory. She is a guardian of the underworld and a guide in visionary space and appears frequently in plant medicine ceremonies to cleanse, teach, and lead us toward deeper healing. Her ability to shed her skin mirrors the integration process itself; we shed what no longer serves and thereby reveal a truer, freer self beneath.

In the Andean tradition, there is *Amaru*, a cosmic serpent who moves between the worlds and represents the power of the *Uku Pacha*, the inner or lower world. This serpent is not merely a creature of the past or the unconscious but a sacred bridge between realms. Often depicted as a winged or two-headed serpent, Amaru embodies paradox and unity, bringing together dualities: earth and sky, death and life, shadow and light. In the Andean trilogy, the serpent walks with the puma (*Kay Pacha*) and condor (*Hanan Pacha*) as part of the full human journey. Integration in this framework is not about bypassing the underworld or aspiring only to spirit, but rather it is about learning to move fluidly through all realms of being.

Both serpents, though arising from different Indigenous cultures, reflect the same universal spiral of transformation that lies at the heart of sacred plant medicine work. We sit in a circle because the circle itself is medicine. It holds each person equally, with no one above or below. The circle is a mirror of the cosmos and a container for sacred space. And like the *ouroboros*, the ancient image of a serpent eating its own tail, the circle reflects the truth that healing is cyclical, not linear. The end is always a new beginning.

Many years ago, during a dieta in the Peruvian Amazon, I had a serpent visit my *tambo* (a tambo is an open-air casita that we stay in on dieta). The serpent was very large, six to eight feet long, and was coiled above my bed in the rafters. I had been resting there on my bed with a thin cotton mosquito net blocking my view of my guest, while I waited for my shaman to bring me medicine for a solo journey. When he arrived, I sat on the stoop talking to him after taking my dose, and at some point in our conversation, his assistant called him over waving and gesturing. He looked up and saw the snake and immediately rushed me out of my tambo saying, "Arani, you have a serpent there, look." He herded me to Samir's tambo, which was along a stream, and when we approached, he shouted to Samir, "She is sleeping with a serpent!" We all laughed, and my adrenaline abated. I landed in Samir's hammock and the medicine immediately came on very strong. I spent the next hours curled up in a ball in absolute terror without any context and all I could do was cry out, "Oh God, help me, help me please!" Samir held the space by gently singing icaros and rattling to support. When I finally started to come down, Samir, who had also taken medicine that day started purging and purging and I picked up the rattle and sang to him. Our guide had his workers move the snake and later that day when Samir asked if it would come back, he replied, "Only if it is lonely."

It is my understanding that the helpless terror I felt that day came from the beginning of my journey in this life, and that Samir's purging was ancestral. All the work we had done to get to that day, that ceremony, invited us to circle back to the very roots of the pain and fear within us and work there. Our coiled serpent visitor symbolically and literally ushered in the continuation of the never-ending journey that is healing. The medicine and the serpent worked together to relocate me to Samir's tambo; if I'd experienced that primal, dark and seemingly never-ending terror on my own in my isolated tambo, it would have been completely overwhelming and beyond my ability to move through. With Samir's presence and gentle support, I was able to stay with the fear and release it. Likewise, the purging that Samir experienced was epic and felt ancient, and my singing encouraged him to let go and trust in the release.

When we understand the serpent and the circle together, we see that integration is not a destination but a returning to self. Life becomes the sacred temple. Each step becomes the ceremony. And the sacred work continues through how we choose to live.

It's important to understand that your integration is cyclical in nature and that within each breath, each moment, each day, our internal worlds are also cyclical. We experience our life, death, and rebirth in our own beings every moment. Each inhalation of breath is connected to life, our birth, and each exhalation of breath is connected to release, letting go, and death. We are connected to Mother Earth and her rhythms; we are intrinsically bound to her and are subject to her in all ways. Our integration journey is one of bringing awareness to the duality in our lives and thereby alchemizing this experience to a more connected whole. Our life energy is the energy of the snake and in our integration process we want to work with it first by bringing awareness to it and then consciously moving it.

The Spiral Within: A Living Ceremony

In many ancient spiritual traditions, the body is the sacred landscape where transformation unfolds. Ancient yogis taught that the dormant force of *kundalini*, which is depicted as a serpent coiled at the base of the spine, represents the deep intelligence of life energy itself waiting to awaken. When stirred, kundalini rises through our central channel, weaving upward through the chakras in a dynamic, spiraling flow. Though often described as an ascent, this energy doesn't move in a straight line. It follows a spiral path, coiling and uncoiling, much like the natural rhythms of nature herself:

there are times of growth, times of blossoming, times of releasing, and times of rest.

This spiral mirrors the journey of integration after ceremony. Just as the kundalini serpent rises in waves, sometimes fierce, sometimes gentle, the path of living what you've experienced through plant medicine is rarely linear. Understandings may come months or years later in unexpected forms. An understanding born in ceremony may take years to fully root in your daily actions. The awakening that happens in visionary states needs space to settle in order to cycle through the layers of your being. Integration is not a finish line; it's a returning, again and again, to the wisdom with new depth, compassion, and embodiment.

In this way, life becomes the real ceremony: a space where energy is always rising, circling, folding back, and moving forward. Whether through inquiry, meditation, breathwork, relating, feeling grief, or showing up for ourselves and others by completing practical tasks, we are invited to constantly spiral toward deeper wholeness. Like the kundalini serpent or the sacred serpents of the Amazon and Andes, we are invited to shed our skins again and again—not to become someone else—but to become more fully ourselves. Integration, then, is not something to complete. It is something to live, to breathe, and to honor—inwardly and outwardly—as a sacred spiral that never truly ends.

The Sacred Spiral and Rhythmic Vibration

In my community in the Amazon, our ceremony circle contains the vibration of the sacred medicine. First, we start in silence and deep listening to connect to the plant spirit internally. Then we increase the vibration, creating friction with music that invites the healing and widening of our consciousness. The healing vibration is strong, omnipresent and powerful. As we increase the intensity, we invite energies that might be scary, intense, challenging or strong, that require our willingness to release, to tap into our courage and our strength. After a time, we shift the energy to a softer more soothing musical vibration to invite rest and breath, then we increase intensity again. There is a rhythm of intensity, rest, intensity, and toward the end sharing and celebration where we come back into our normal consciousness. We close with a ritual that includes lighting a candle and expressing gratitude, sending the plants, spirits, ancestors, deities, enlightened beings, animals back home and honoring the Four Directions.

The vibrational energy of the ceremony is an energy force that connects each participant, and each participant is a part of the whole. No ceremony is ever alike, each ceremony unfolds perfectly, and each participant is an essential part of this sacred dance.

Use this metaphor for your integration journey: including periods of silence, periods of intensity, periods of rest, periods of celebration, taking space and coming back into the circle. Allow space for each vibration, each energy within your being to be experienced. If you practice this in integration, then you have a path to follow also for your life. You can't go back. You can try to forget, but some part of you is longing to heal and remember, otherwise you would not have been in ceremony in the first place. You might as well commit to continuing the journey intentionally.

Attuning to the Vibration of Ceremony in Everyday Life

We can make our routine tasks a ritual just by bringing presence to them. The ceremony of our life can then become a series of rituals that we intentionally move through in our day-to-day world: walking the talk; chopping wood; carrying water.

If we can start to grasp the significance of how miraculous it is that we are here, in this human form in this time and space, and approach our lives as such, our lives become the ceremony. We open and close each day with intention and gratitude. In the middle we move through the myriads of vibrations of our days with the courage to release what no longer serves, be present with what is, detach from future expectations, and do our best. This is where the real transformation can take root: in the ceremony of life.

We start with creating space to allow the vibration, the energy of healing, to be felt. In this book we will first explore the outer layers and move inward, then circle back, as in a sacred spiral. The journey is infinite and just like in a ceremony it is circular, with a cadence, a rhythm, ongoing, as is the wheel of life. Just one step at a time. Many of the self-exploration exercises in this book might seem simple, perhaps too simple. As I'm sure you will find, simple does not mean easy. Persistence and a willingness to explore is important here. Meaning and wisdom come from experience, so this is an invitation for you to experience *yourself*. You can read the words, but the real meaning will come through the experiential use of the materials provided.

> *"I beg you, to have patience with everything unresolved in your heart and to try to love the questions themselves as if they were locked rooms or books written in a very foreign language. Don't search for the answers, which could not be given to you now, because you would not be able to live them. And the point is to live everything. Live the questions now. Perhaps then, someday far in the future, you will gradually, without even noticing it, live your way into the answer."*
>
> —Rainer Maria Rilke

Let's start with a few journal prompts for you to explore.

Journal Reflection Prompts: Bringing The Sacred Home

What moments in my day feel most alive, present, or sacred *in their simplicity*?

What if integration isn't something to complete, but a way of living in presence?

Reflect on how shifting your mindset from this is an *outcome-oriented energy* to *this is an ongoing journey energy* changes how you relate to your ceremony integration.

An integrated person is one who takes agency from the inner landscape. A disintegrated person is one who acts from the outer landscape. Explore your understanding of this statement now.

Chapter Two: The Quiet Power of Intention

"At the center of your being you have the answer; you know who you are and you know what you want."

—Lao Tzu

Personal Intentions

Let's circle back to the beginning of your journey. Did you set an intention before you participated in a medicine ceremony? If so, revisiting that intention is a good way to reconnect with it to support your integration process. In my work supporting people preparing to experience sacred plant medicines, I encourage them to set an intention as part of their preparation work. Setting an intention is a way to prepare and focus on why you are attending the ceremony. It helps create discipline around other preparations such as honoring the dietary guidelines, creating space, and self-care. If you did not set an intention, think back to why you wanted to attend the ceremony. Revisit and feel into what intentions were present within you.

Intentions are very personal. Looking at them helps us to understand where we were when we entered our journey and what we thought we needed to receive. Our personal intentions that got us to ceremony—whether it be to heal, explore, or expand—are also the framework for our integration.

That being said, the sacred plant medicines are intelligent in ways that we cannot grasp in our three-dimensional field. Often in my work with people on their integration journey, they share that they had a clear intention to work on a particular issue, and they found themselves somewhere else entirely. Much to their surprise, they felt that this was exactly what was needed for them, and they felt seen and understood in a deep and meaningful way by the plant spirits. I can't tell you how many times I've heard people say, "I thought I was here to look at this relationship or this pattern, and instead I found myself way over there. Now I realize this is exactly where I needed to be, and I feel so blessed to be shown the way."

Plant medicine meets us where we are and shows us what we are ready to heal and understand. Remembering our personal intentions is useful to begin our integration journey as a reminder of why we are here and where we are now in seeking integration.

Journal Reflection Prompts: Intentions

What was my intention going into ceremony, and how has it evolved since the experience? Has it deepened, shifted, or revealed new layers?

Now distill your current integration intention into one simple sentence. Write this sentence down and display it somewhere as a reminder of that which you are longing to explore, heal, or understand.

Holding our personal intentions, let's explore now through a wider lens.

Healing and Self-Knowledge as Our Sacred Foundation

In the Indigenous Amazonian tradition that I am a part of, it's said that sacred plant medicine is used for two things: healing and self-knowledge. I like the seeming simplicity of this intention, and I have reminded myself many times when my fear or pain seems unbearable that this is the work, this is my path, and this is why I am here.

I say seeming simplicity because healing and self-knowledge are multifaceted and multilayered quests and journeys of a thousand lifetimes. For the purposes of integrating a plant medicine journey we start with these principles because these are the cornerstones of our integration journeys.

Generally, every human who finds themselves participating in plant medicine ceremony is showing up to work on themselves. We as humans want to feel better, we want to like ourselves more, be less angry or fearful, experience connection, and feel whole.

Using the cornerstones of healing and self-knowledge, you create guideposts for your integration. We are not trying to box your experience in, but rather trying to offer language through which to interpret and understand your experience. If you think of your integration as a journey, you can think of healing and self-knowledge as guideposts that will support your whole being.

For now, healing can be understood as the courage to feel our pain, anger, and other emotions without judgement but with awareness and compassion. Self-knowledge is the inner process of peeling back the layers of conditionings and adaptations to experience our true selves that lie dormant and forgotten within us. Both healing and self-knowledge are journeys of self-discovery: mysteries to be lived and alchemized.

In this book we explore ways of experiencing healing and self-knowledge to support your integration. I suggest that in addition to your personal intention that we explored above, you also use the understanding that your experience's guideposts are healing and self-knowledge. Understanding your plant medicine experience as a healing journey and a journey of self-knowing creates a positive foundation that will support you. With this understanding you are in alignment with and in sync with the stewards of the plants for millennia: the wisdom keepers, the sacred plants themselves, and Mother Earth (*Pachamama*.)

Before you go any further in this book, explore this understanding: whatever your experience was, allow the idea that it was anchored in healing and self-knowledge to take root in your being. This is an understanding that will help you feel calm and centered.

Journal Reflection Prompts: Healing and Self Knowledge

What does healing mean to me in relationship with myself? What needs attention? What needs to be let go of?

What am I curious about in terms of my own inner world and how it impacts the way I see myself and my life?

After looking at our personal intentions and the wider Indigenous lens of healing and self-knowledge, let's widen our lens further by exploring overarching themes that we experience through sacred plant medicine journeys.

The Collective Mirror: Common Themes in Sacred Ceremony

When approaching integration, it's helpful to understand that your unique experience is also connected to a larger whole. Understanding your experience with sacred plant medicines as a vibration, an intelligence beyond the mind and connected to the whole, brings a sense of being a part of the mystery that is this life. Although each journey is unique, knowing that fellow travelers share similar otherworldly, mystical experiences can help us to ground and connect to the experience more deeply. Each medicine journey is personal, but there are certain universal themes that tend to permeate.

"Time is a continuity which overlaps itself. Its rear is coupled to its van. Nothing is ended and dismissed in Time; and nothing is begun and finished."

—Mikhail Naimy

The first time I drank ayahuasca, I had traveled down to the jungle in Peru. We—my partner Samir and I—had been invited a few months before by a friend while celebrating his birthday in California. The medicine path was not on my radar at that time, and we were planning a trip to India later that year. When our friend told us about his experience, my initial response was literally: *not interested*. Over the course of hosting people in his home our friend appeared to be a bit stressed, and I remember thinking, "If this is the result of such an experience, I'll stick with my meditation practice." Ha. However, on the plane ride home from California, I opened a book I had brought along by Isabella Allende, *The Sum of Our Days: A Memoir.*[3]

I had started it a few years before and so opened it on the bookmarked page where I had left off. In this very chapter, on this very page, she described wanting to connect with her maternal lineage and the magic of her *abuelas* in order to share it with her grandchildren. She then commenced to describe her journey to South America and her experience there with the sacred plant medicine, ayahuasca. I was quite astonished and also deeply moved, and I asked Samir if this was indeed what our friend had been referring to. When he said yes, I knew that I had to go. It was so clear. The medicine invites its guests. The medicine is in charge of its trajectory in the world.

On my first journey, I arrived in South America for a traditional dieta having no idea what to expect. Upon our arrival at the camp in the jungle, our curandero had asked Samir and I how many times we had drank the medicine. When we said none, he laughed out loud, boomingly and pointed at us in mirth. The joke was on us.

In my first ceremony, it took a while for the medicine to come on. I remember hearing purging and crying in the dark and wondering why I wasn't experiencing these things. The music was incredible. I was very worried that I wasn't feeling altered, so when I heard a call to receive more medicine I scooted up to the altar without trepidation, that feeling of being left out egging me on. For the record, that is the last time I have ever moved to receive medicine at the altar without trepidation.

Almost immediately after that, time stopped. What I remember is finding myself at the bed of my dying Dutch grandmother, Effie. I was talking to her and rubbing her cold feet, telling her how much I loved her, how much she meant to me, and how grateful I was to have her be my grandma. I was there with her, holding her and reassuring her, supporting her transition. It was real to me. I was there, back through time. Later in my journey, I was

3 Allende, Isabel. *The Sum of Our Days: A Memoir*. Translated by Margaret Sayers Peden. New York: Harper, 2008.

lying on the earth in the very jungle where our ceremony took place. I felt held and supported by Pachamama, Mother Earth, as I felt my spirit releasing into the oneness that is existence. So many tears streamed down my face; and I had the experience of them watering Pachamama, being absorbed into her warm embrace and transmuted into new life. This experience was beyond words—and even as I share the story here—I cannot accurately describe the beauty of this moment where time did not exist, and I was held so lovingly in Pachamama's embrace.

I was nineteen when my Grandma Effie died. When I arrived at her bedside to say goodbye, a woman I didn't know was hovering over her. In my grief and confusion, I didn't have the strength or clarity to ask her to step aside to make space for me. So, I hung back. When my grandma asked, "Where is my beautiful granddaughter?" I whispered, "I'm right here, Grandma," and then I started crying and left the room. I never held her hand, never thanked her, never told her I loved her. Shortly after, my mom asked me to take my younger cousins home and stay with them. I did. That was it. My grandma died later that night.

Her passing left me with a profound grief—not only for her death—but for that moment I hadn't been able to thank her for her presence in my life. She was the grandmother who took my brother and I every Saturday night, read to us until her voice was hoarse, taught me to sew and craft, and took us to Sunday school. She was an anchor in my early life, a steady and loving presence when I felt utterly unmoored, unloved, and unwanted. I had buried the memory of that final moment at her bedside and didn't realize how deeply it had shaped me. The echo of her voice asking, "Where is my granddaughter?" haunted me. That unspoken goodbye lived on in my body and unconscious mind.

To find myself with her again, across time, held by the medicine was incredibly healing. The medicine knows. It shows us what we most need to see, to feel, to heal.

Time, death, the archetype of the mother, Pachamama, subconscious and unconscious memories, unity, nature, spirituality, all danced together on my first journey. There is no need for me to try to make meaning or question the reality of this gift. I experienced it. That ceremony gave me a gift of such magnitude, one that traced many of the universal themes and teachings these medicines offer. Let's explore these themes here now.

Ego Dissolution

Ego dissolution and a sense of unity or oneness is a recurring theme in plant medicine journeys, particularly with ayahuasca. When our consciousness expands, we feel boundaries soften or disappear and we experience a sense of unity with existence, nature, and the universe. Here we might lose our sense of being an individual and our sense of identity (ego). For some, this experience can feel absolutely horrifying, while for others it can feel quite liberating. Either way it is a temporary state that often feels elusive and confusing as we try to reorient in our ordinary lives.

Death and Rebirth

Death and rebirth are another common theme. Many plant medicine journeys include a sense of being plunged or trapped in darkness and then reemerging into light. These journeys mirror the psychological process of alchemy that we will explore in Chapter Sixteen. Sometimes journeyers experience and find themselves witnessing or holding the deaths of loved ones in a new way. Other times, it is parts of ourselves that must die, or perhaps old ways of being that we're ready to release. Death and rebirth are a central motif in ceremonies, just as in nature. Ayahuasca is known as the "vine of the dead," and one of its main traditional purposes is to prepare us for death and teach us how to die consciously (as with all the other wisdom traditions).

Past Lives

Along these lines, journeyers may receive glimpses or threads of insight into past lives. These experiences can offer a window into karmic patterns that continue to play out in this lifetime. When approached with discernment and care, we can understand that they are not meant to become new identities for the mind to cling to. Instead, when properly integrated, they can guide us toward healing, understanding, and releasing what no longer serves us here and now.

Subconscious Memories

Subconscious or suppressed memories can also resurface in these ceremonies. Plant medicines can act as magnifiers of subconscious suppressed memories, repressed emotions, or unresolved relationships. Becoming aware of our subconscious minds and suppressed memories can be very healing if approached with compassion and awareness. Meeting your inner child, experiencing deep unprocessed grief, understanding an experience that helped shape your adaptive patterns: all are often a part of the journey. Working with these memories, both in the ceremony and in integration, can help alchemize them into healing. The medicine is in essence inviting us to release, integrate, and heal.

Connection to Earth

Our connection to Mother Earth is another gift of plant medicine ceremony. Nature experienced as an animated living presence and intelligence allows a new and deeper understanding of the natural world. We become aware that nature is alive and supporting us all the time. Trees may appear conscious, rivers may speak, animals encountered may radiate wisdom. In our journeys we sense this with our emotional and somatic bodies and realize that we are not above nature, nor are we separate from nature, but an intrinsic part of her.

Archetypes

Archetypes can arise in plant medicine journeys. Psychedelic states tap into the collective unconscious, revealing patterns of the human psyche. Archetypal energies or forms such as the wise old woman, the trickster, the Divine Mother, the inner child, the victim, the martyr, the prostitute, the miser, etc., all may manifest in ceremony to teach us about who we are and how we move in the world. These experiences connect us to something ancestral and eternal that transcends our individual lives and helps us to realize that we are part of something much bigger than these tiny bodies we call home.

Shifts in Time and Space

Sacred plant medicine experiences frequently involve experiencing radical alterations of time and space. Minutes may feel like hours, or entire lifetimes may be lived in one night. Visiting other dimensions, perceiving multiple timelines simultaneously, finding oneself back in another time or ahead in an unknown future challenge our conventional understanding of reality and leave a lasting impact. We may come away from our experience with the sense that there is no such thing as time. Now what?

Connection to the Divine

Spirituality is, of course, often a cornerstone of sacred plant journeys. Journeyers might experience a profound sense of the divine in many ways through many different forms and faces. These experiences can create a deep sense of awe, gratitude, and humility. The medicine opens a window into the mystery that is existence. This is perhaps the most deeply felt resonance offered by these ceremonies: the spiritual dimension of our journeys. Across space, place and time for millennia, sacred plants have opened altered states of consciousness that serve as portals to the divine—not in the abstract but in the felt, lived sense—through the experience of an energy vibration greater or wiser than us, yet also a part of us. In ceremony, when the layers of identity peel away, what remains often is the sacred center[4] which is a place beyond language where truth resides within us. We experience this as unshakably real, perhaps more real than our ordinary lives.

The journey doesn't end when we close the ceremony. In fact, that is where the real work begins. Integration, the alchemy of transforming and healing what is received into life, requires discipline. If we can apply a little friction to our beings then the sacred plant ceremony does not become just an event in our life but rather a vibration, a fluid energy, that guides us onward long after the ceremony. Integration then is a journey to live the ceremony, honor the mystery, and sacred nature of the medicine received. Each

4 In this book we will be exploring our sacred center in depth. When I reference it, I am referring to the place within us where the inner fire and wisdom of our navel center and our subtle minds are online and in sync.

plant journey is a miracle. A gift from the beyond. A mystery to be lived. This book is an invitation to remember this and embody it.

With our personal intention and two guideposts of healing and self-knowledge, the next step is to understand how healing and self-knowledge work within our beings. First, we do not heal through our thinking minds. We heal as whole beings and our bodies store that which needs to be healed. Our minds carry our stories, and our stories are based on our interpretations of our experiences. Our bodies carry our actual experiences and hold them for us until we are able and courageous enough to fully process them.

Any journey worth having has challenges and in the plant medicine realm we are often surprised at how our physical bodies are such a big part of our experiences. We might feel pain in areas of our bodies and not understand why; find ourselves purging forcefully in our bucket or on the toilet; find ourselves frozen and unable to move or speak; shaking, sweating, feeling very cold or very warm; or feeling our bodies as separate and far away. Each journey is influenced by how the body is experienced. Our minds are diligently trying to define, dismiss, or delineate our experience into a narrative that makes sense. This is a part of integration, and we will come to it in the next chapters. For now, we have our guideposts: our personal intentions, healing and self-knowledge and next we want to find the beginning of our path.

Chapter Three:

Grounding Ourselves After Ceremony

"Out beyond ideas of wrongdoing and right doing, there is a field. I'll meet you there."

—Rumi

One of the most important elements of your ceremony integration is grounding yourself once you return home. With the understanding that your integration is unfolding in its own rhythm, the first step to support this process is to ensure that you are steady in your practical world and the choices you are making right now, today. Approach this with the same sense of intention that you brought to your ceremony.

Show Up in Your Real World

Grounding is the sacred return to the body, breath, and the tasks that tether us to the Earth. As the old Zen saying goes, "Before enlightenment, chop wood, carry water. After enlightenment, chop wood, carry water." This simple phrase, rooted in Zen Buddhist tradition, reminds us that no matter how expansive or visionary our inner experiences may be, true integration happens through ordinary life. Washing dishes, walking barefoot, tending the garden, making tea: these become rituals of remembrance. Grounding is not a descent from spirit, but a way to embody it.

You have responsibilities in the real world that need attention, such as paying your bills, watering your plants, maintaining your home, and showing up at work. These responsibilities include practical self-care, including grounding after ceremony. Showing up in the day-to-day reality of your life and giving the energy required to sustain it on a practical level is an important part of the integration journey. Allow these responsibilities to stabilize you. When we take care of our practical day-to-day responsibilities, we create a sense of inner capability that allows our nervous system to reset and to rest.

In my life, I like to think of these practical responsibilities as "chopping wood and carrying water." Sometimes, when I feel completely overwhelmed and unsure of what to do in terms of my practical affairs, I do laundry. I have this motto: when in doubt, do laundry. Taking action allows energy to start flowing. I like laundry. I like gathering and sorting and the buzz of the machines as they clean the clothes. I like getting them out of the dryer and folding them and then putting them away. It's a small task that feels satisfying. My fear and overwhelm are not interested in my laundry tasks, and so these tasks bring comfort to me, as I move my energy in this tactile, practical way.

I suggest you create your own when in doubt activity. I have found that creating this simple movement releases the feeling of being overwhelmed, stuck, frozen, and translates into more action. By starting with the laundry, my own when-in-doubt task, I find that I create momentum, and the next thing I know, the kitchen is clean, I've changed the sheets, the plants are watered, etc. I feel grounded in my ordinary world, competent and capable. Find your when in doubt task. I think that you too will find that reorienting toward the practical mundane aspects of life will bring a sense of balance to you. Many friends who experience entheogens feel that they need space to integrate their experience, separate from their ordinary lives, such as by disappearing to a silent retreat, doing weeks of yoga and breathwork, or retreating into isolation with journals and spiritual books. In my experience these spaces just require further integration. Integration doesn't happen when we reject our ordinary lives, rather it is supported by our ordinary lives as we approach them with a new reverence.

I once had an integration session with a woman who said she was having a very hard time landing. I asked her how she was grounding herself and she said she was listening to the music of ceremony and fasting because she wanted to keep the plant medicine vibration going within her. I gently explained to her that the plant medicine vibration did not need this separation but rather needed her embodied presence in her current life.

"Wash every bowl, every dish, as if you are bathing the baby Buddha—breathing in, feeling joy; breathing out, smiling. Every minute can be a holy, sacred minute. Where do you seek the spiritual? You seek the spiritual in every ordinary thing that you do every day. Sweeping the floor, watering the vegetables, and washing the dishes become holy and sacred if mindfulness is there. With mindfulness and concentration, everything becomes spiritual."

—Thich Nhat Hanh

Rest!

As important as it is to move energy in your practical world, it is equally as important to allow space. Quiet. Rest. Regardless of how demanding your practical responsibilities are, feeling grounded also requires that we find time for activities that are quiet, allow stillness, and that nurture us. Rest is an essential part of the integration process, offering space for the body, mind, and spirit to settle and assimilate deep inner work. Just as nature honors cycles of rest, trees shed their leaves, the earth lies fallow in winter, and animals retreat into hibernation, our healing also needs time to pause and restore. In these quiet moments, our understandings deepen, our nervous systems recalibrate, and the possibility of transformation roots itself more fully. Rest isn't passive; it's a sacred rhythm that allows growth to take hold. By rest I mean *not doing*—napping or sitting in nature—and I also mean non-goal-oriented activities that allow energy to flow, like dancing or playing music for pleasure.

Simple practices that invite energy to move and support grounding can be very helpful. Instead of ruminating and wondering about our experience, which if overdone can become self-indulgent, inviting creativity and playfulness into the integration process is important. Shutting down our energy by losing our selves to distractions such as screen time and social media news feeds is not so supportive Breaking these habits by experimenting with other ways of spending down time can create a sense of self care and spaciousness. Make art. Spend time in nature. Be playful. We tend to take ourselves very seriously and this creates tension.

Grounding through Movement and Creativity

I encourage you to explore yoga, dance, or other forms of movement as a part of your integration. These practices free energy in the body and can be done either at home or by attending group classes. At home just put on some music and dance or sign up for a local movement class. Movement can be so freeing and it's so good for your energy to create flow in this way.

Engage in creative expression such as drawing, painting, writing poetry or expressing yourself with free writing,

Another creative and fun activity that supports integration is to design or color mandalas to access symbolic insight and bring balance to your inner world. Mandalas are found in both Eastern spiritual traditions and in American Indigenous traditions. Mandalas are considered symbolic representations of the process of spiritual evolution. You can either create your own mandala or use adult coloring books with predesigned mandalas. Your mandala can become a tangible representation of your experience, and it can be a subtle reminder if placed visibly within your home, allowing you to stay in contact with your journey. Not surprisingly, Carl Jung attributes the circular shape of the mandala to the archetype of self, representing the totality of the psyche and its parts. In essence the mandala is a representation of wholeness. What a wonderful creative tool to work with during integration. I have a dear friend who works with materials from nature to create mandalas with flowers, leaves, twigs, rocks, etc. and this becomes her sacred altar. It's beautiful to behold and is symbolic of her intention, her journey and her love of nature.

Mandalas are universal images of sacred wholeness. It is wonderful to work with them during integration, either by creating your own or by finding images to color.

Similar to creating or coloring mandalas is collage making. Create mixed media art using images, textures, or colors to represent your inner journey. Creating a collage is a super fun way to move creatively, whether you use old magazines, cards, fabrics, buttons, or found objects. Being in the creative flow by cutting and pasting and allowing abstract expression can be an excellent resource for yourself. You might be surprised at how cool and informative the collage turns out.

Expressing through the voice is incredibly supportive to integration. Learning mantras or songs and using our voices *out loud* can be so healing and connecting. If you've never worked with mantra there are many beautiful sacred chants that can be learned and then practiced, depending on what your intentions are. Healing mantras, songs of inspiration, fun songs that rock your spirit are all equally supportive. If songs and sacred mantras are not familiar allies, I've shared some in the resources section at the back of this book for you to experiment with. Finding our voice, hearing our own voice sing out loud, sharing our voice can be so healing, especially for those of us who do not think we are musically inclined.

In that vein, playing music is deeply nourishing during integration. Many friends are inspired to learn to play a musical instrument for the first time or learn a new instrument after ceremony and this then becomes a gift that continues in their lives.

We can also work with Tarot & oracle cards. Draw cards for insight, reflection and guidance. Let images and symbols express messages from the deeper self. This can be a playful activity as well. These can be a fun way to look at your life and inner work from a different perspective. At one point in my journey before plant medicine, I was in the depths of a painful process that seemed never-ending, and a friend suggested that we draw my animal card totem. The cards brought such relief, laughter, and joy into the moment. I still have the totem and refer to it upon occasion. My mountain lion, black panther, hummingbird, opossum, etc. are all supporting me here now.

Staying Grounded: Practice Discernment

In seeking to ground yourself, practice discernment. Not every insight or vision from your ceremony needs to be acted upon literally. In fact, it's recommended that any major life change such as a move, divorce, or a new job should not be made until at least a few months after the ceremony. Be mindful of the energies around you in your home and work life and discern whether they are supportive to you. If they are not supportive or you are not sure, consider taking a pause from these energies for now. Take care to make sure that you place yourself in spaces that will nurture you and your experience and that won't cause you to regress and lose traction. Do this without judgment. You don't need to explain or rationalize these choices or decisions. Be discerning.

Staying Grounded: Leaking

It is also important for you to not leak your process. Integration is an inner journey and so trying to describe it in detail or make meaning with others can short circuit the fuller, more subtle experience that is still unfolding. By containing your process, you are creating space to listen to your own wisdom, to feel what needs to be felt and to heal what is coming into the light to be healed. Share as it feels right with discernment and remember that making meaning and narrative moves our experience into our mind's realm and may create a defined outcome that will then cause the ongoing vibration of the healing to be lost.

Returning To Earth: Grounding Through Nature

Connecting to nature is so important. Taking a long hike or spending time in a park, feeling the sun on your skin, taking your shoes off and feeling the sacred Pachamama beneath your feet, are all gifts to yourself that can nourish your sense of connection. Use your senses: listen to the birds sing, see the leaves on the trees, smell the pine needles, touch the bark of the tree and feel its quiet grace. Invite connection to the earth by sensing its support of your body whether standing, sitting, or lying down. Try breathing gently with your eyes closed, feel your internal roots expanding and connecting downward to meet the roots of the plants and trees below the surface.

On a walk, you might see a beautiful rock. You might pause in appreciation and run your fingers over its surface, perhaps feeling the cool moss growing on it. When clouds move across the sky, you might pause; watch them drift, maybe dance on the earth beneath them, or lie down and simply let them pass overhead. In time, as you grow quieter inside, you may feel them moving not only through the outer sky but through your own inner being. The boundary between you and the world isn't real. You become aware that you are no longer separate. You are the sky, and the sky is you.

Indeed, nature is a resource that is so supportive and healing. Nature can awaken our reverence for our life and all lives. Its beauty can inspire us to be creative and awaken our eternal sense of gratitude for life. Spending time in nature connects us to the natural rhythm of creation of which we are an intrinsic part. It's a sanctuary from our busy modern lives and connecting to it in this way expands our presence and sense of connection to the whole. Nature is healing. It is always in flow. Let it teach you to slow down and move softly.

"You carry mother earth within you. She is not outside of you. Mother Earth is not just your environment. In that insight of inner-being, it is possible to have real communication with the earth, which is the highest form of prayer."

—Thich Nhat Han

Breathwork/Asana Practice: Simple Natural Breathing

Sitting in sukhasana with hands in Buddha mudra cultivates a contained energy field, fostering internal circulation and preventing energy leakage, which enhances deep inner connection.

Conscious breathing is another helpful and supportive tool in your integration tool kit. To practice, sit in a comfortable position with your hands resting gently on your lap. Put your hands in Buddha mudra with right hand cupped in left hand and thumbs touching and rest them on your lap. This is a posture that has been cultivated by the wisdom keepers for millennia and it is understood that in this posture all the energy within becomes circular and doesn't leak out. Make sure your spine is straight by lifting your heart and tucking your chin ever so slightly. Relax your shoulders so that they slide down. Inhale and exhale through your nostrils in a relaxed comfortable rhythm. Keep your eyes closed and try to roll them so that they are directed at the point between your two brows or your third eye *drishti* (point of concentration). Focus on your breath. Notice the rhythm of your breath. Bring attention to the breath in your body as your lungs expand with each inhale and contract with each exhale. Practice tuning into your breath repeatedly to reconnect to it. Your mind and nervous system will follow your breath making this a great way to regulate, just by tuning in consciously. You might start by setting your timer for three minutes and then extending this time to eleven minutes. Meditative music can be supportive.

Feeling grounded is important and tuning in is key. We need to feel rooted in our lives. If you feel agitated or ungrounded you can develop an internal dialogue by coming back to your natural breath and asking yourself: what do I need? What would support me here, now? Perhaps a walk, journaling, some food, music, rest...

"To be rooted is perhaps the most important and least recognized need of the human soul."

—Simone Weil

Chapter Four:

Integration Means Integrity

The word integration comes from the Latin word *integrāre*, meaning to make whole. It shares its root with integrity, which refers to a state of wholeness, honesty, and alignment. In the context of healing and sacred plant work, integration is not simply about receiving medicine, attending ceremony, and identifying as a medicine person; it's about embodying the experience in our ordinary lives. It is the journey of aligning our inner truths with our outer actions, so that how we live reflects who we are.

To integrate an experience is to weave it into the fabric of our daily life. To live with integrity means we honor that weaving process by staying connected to our authenticity, even when it's uncomfortable or inconvenient. Both require a return to self and an ongoing inquiry into what is aligned with us and what is no longer needed.

Integration without integrity is impossible, theoretical, and acts as a collection of ideas that become our new identities with no lived change. But integration with integrity is transformation. It allows our healing and growth to take root not just in our minds, but in our very beings. Then our lives become the ceremony.

Working with The Four Agreements for Inner Integrity

One of the deepest invitations of the integration process is to live in greater integrity with ourselves. This means aligning our inner truth with our outer actions. One timeless guide for this kind of embodied integrity comes from *The Four Agreements,* drawn from Toltec wisdom and popularized by Don Miguel Ruiz. These agreements offer practical, spiritual wisdom that supports authenticity, clear boundaries, and integration. I read this book just last year as I travelled home from Peru. I had picked it up at the airport hotel and thought to finally explore it, as I had heard about it for many years. I found it refreshing in its wisdom and practical simplicity and I summarize it here, as it epitomizes walking in integrity.[5]

1. **Be Impeccable with Your Word**
   This first agreement reminds us that language shapes our reality. In integration, this means speaking truthfully to ourselves and others. Being impeccable includes honoring the understandings that surfaced during ceremony, naming our needs, and avoiding self-judgment. When our words are clear, kind, and congruent, they become a tool for healing rather than harm.

2. **Don't Take Anything Personally**
   During integration, emotional sensitivity can increase. This agreement teaches us that others' behavior is a reflection of their reality, not a definition of our worth. It invites emotional boundaries and helps reduce the inner chaos caused by projecting meaning onto others' actions. When we stop personalizing everything, we reclaim our energy and stay grounded in our own path.

3. **Don't Make Assumptions**
   Plant medicines often reveal how much of our suffering

5 Ruiz, Don Miguel. *The Four Agreements: A Practical Guide to Personal Freedom*. San Rafael, CA: Amber-Allen Publishing, 1997.

comes from mental narratives and false interpretations. This agreement encourages us to pause, ask questions, and clarify instead of filling in the blanks with old stories. In practice, this looks like curiosity over reactivity. It's a vital part of integrating within ourselves and eases the way we relate with others.

4. **Always Do Your Best**
   This is the agreement that allows room for the spiraling and circular rhythm of integration. Doing our best allows us to honor wherever we find ourselves in our journey. Integration isn't about improving ourselves, but about showing up fully, honestly, and compassionately and working with what is coming up for us without forcing, comparing, or shaming ourselves.

Together, these agreements become a daily compass and a way to bring ceremony wisdom into everyday living. They support integrity not as a rigid ideal, but as a living expression of integration with self. To be in integrity with the whole we first have to find our own personal, inner integrity.

Integrity and Cultural Appropriation

After attending an Indigenous ceremony, especially as a non-Indigenous participant, it is essential to carry the experience with deep humility, respect, and discernment. These ceremonies are sacred, rooted in generations of lived experience, oral tradition, and community practices that extend far beyond our own individual healing journey. A danger that can emerge after such powerful experiences is the unconscious and well-intentioned but harmful appropriation of Indigenous culture, using symbols, language, rituals, or ceremonial objects outside their proper context or without permission.

Cultural appropriation often stems from a genuine desire to honor what was received. However, when sacred elements are removed from their cultural roots, commodified, or shared without context, they can be stripped of their integrity. This not only disrespects the communities who have safeguarded these practices, often at great cost, but can also contribute to the ongoing colonization and erasure of Indigenous voices and identities. Wearing regalia, using Indigenous language in casual settings, teaching or leading ceremonies without permission, the overharvesting of sacred plants such as *palo santo* and sage, or claiming titles like shaman without invitation, are all actions that can perpetuate harm, even if unintentionally.

For instance, I have been taught that in the traditions of the Amazon, the palo santo tree is a sacred protector and healer capable of removing dark energies, among other things. Traditionally this medicine is harvested by waiting several years after a tree has fallen naturally to honor the spirit of the living deity that is this tree. Only then do the Indigenous people carefully and with great respect harvest the wood to use in ceremony and life for protection and support. Now Westerners have fallen in love with this smudging process and so the trees are felled—living breathing beings, powerful wisdom *maestros*, to satisfy our desire to smudge our homes and yoga studios. The palo santo tree is becoming endangered. What to do?

True integration after Indigenous ceremonies involves listening deeply, not just to the personal experience of the self, but to the voices of the culture and wisdom keepers who have stewarded these medicines for millennia. This means seeking consent before sharing or using any teachings; and redirecting attention and resources toward the communities that have held and protected these lineages. It also means recognizing that not everything experienced is meant to be spoken about or passed on. Respect includes restraint.

The medicine received in Indigenous ceremony often calls us into a higher standard of integrity. This includes acknowledging the responsibility to protect what is sacred, not as owners or transmitters, but as allies. As part of integration, this awareness becomes a practice of walking in integrity with self, with others, with Pachamama.

All of the Indigenous wisdom I share in this book I do so with permission from my teachers to support your connection to the plant medicine and healing. I deeply respect the ancient lineages that I have been so blessed to become a part of. I ask that, as I am sharing this wisdom, you as my reader treat these as sacred teachings and honor them with respect by always thanking the wisdom keepers who have carried them down through time, offering gratitude for the permission to share and support your healing.

And on a deeper level, as a part of my own process in understanding appropriation over the years, I came to recognize a part of my own heritage and DNA. I too have Indigenous roots. My beloved paternal grandfather, Raymond Gonzales, grew up as an impoverished sheep herder in the hills surrounding Las Vegas, New Mexico. His mother, my great-grandmother Juanita, was Indigenous, from the tribes of that region. Though I do not know the exact measure of that heritage within them or from what tribes we came from, I do know that my own DNA reflects that I am eleven-percent Indigenous.

Although my family has been completely severed from any memory or knowledge of this ancestral lineage, I feel the connection in my being and have experienced profound healing around this through plant medicine. I remember my great grandmother, Juanita, as being a very small frail woman, blind and in a wheelchair at a family reunion when I was very young. I never spoke to her or touched her, yet she lives in my heart and blood. I have grieved the loss of this connection through time and distance and colonialization; continue to grieve the treatment of the Indigenous Wisdom Keepers throughout Western civilization; and find balance and pride in not only my Indigenous ancestors but my Dutch, Scottish, and Spanish ancestors as well—and the ancient wisdom keeping traditions they come from. These polarities exist within me and in all of us. I share this not as one claiming Indigenous identity but because even with this connection I am conditioned and live in the Western world; even with this genetic link I have to guard against my own Western tendency to appropriate, to make mine. Empathy, humility, and respect is required in engaging with Indigenous peoples and wisdom traditions. How can I be in right relationship with the Indigenous stewards of the plantas maestras who are my teachers?

This very question arose when I met with my editor and book designer to discuss the cover for this book. I had the idea of using the pattern of the Shipibo-Conibo textiles which depicts the vibration of the icaros. My editor asked if this could be considered appropriation and it stopped me cold. Oh, wow. Since the answer was not clear I let go.

Chapter Five:

Cultivating Connection Through Presence

Now that we've worked on grounding, let's explore connection as another important layer of creating a safe integration container.

"As above, so below; as below, so above."
—The Kybalion

Everything in the universe is energy vibrating at different frequencies. From the vastness of galaxies to the subtle movement of breath, we are part of an interconnected field that pulses with life. In integration, we begin to sense this more deeply, not just as an idea, but as a felt experience. Our thoughts, emotions, and bodies are all expressions of this energy, and when we shift internally, the world around us shifts too. To heal ourselves is to contribute to the healing of the whole, because ultimately, there is no separation. Existence is one. We are energy in motion, woven into the same sacred web.

And yet, we experience ourselves as separate from this oneness. The inner journey of integration is a journey toward this oneness. When we have an experience of divine oneness in ceremony, it's a remembrance that needs nourishment and care. Tending to this oneness within takes tremendous courage because we are required to drop all that we are not. Our identities are our passports through our lives, and we pull them out as we journey on and on in our outer worlds. Traveling inward is more arduous and requires us to leave our passports and all the stamps in it behind. It is our lived experience of being separate from the whole that creates our suffering. We have forgotten so we must remember, recalibrate, and reconnect. In ceremony, when our minds experience a sense of this oneness it makes us realize that there is another possibility for our inner landscape that is more natural to us. We can orient toward this in our integration. With effort, the mind can relax. When the mind is relaxed, we can then be present with the secret and mystery that is just beyond our sensory world, and our hearts can open to compassion. This is integration.

Reclaiming Connection to the Senses

How do we reconnect to this oneness in our busy daily lives? First, we must understand and reconnect with ourselves. Let's start with our senses, as these are our gateway to connection with the outside world. There is an ancient sacred Hindu text known as the *Kaivalya Upanishad*, that starts with this prayer:

> *"Om.*
> *May all the limbs of my body grow strong.*
> *May my speech be nourished and strengthened.*
> *May my nose, my eyes, my ears and my other sense organs*
> *be nourished and strengthened….*
> *Om shanti shanti shanti."*

Interesting that this ancient sacred text starts with this ancient sage, whose name has been forgotten, praying for his outer senses to be strengthened. Why? When we are aware of our senses we are in presence. We can use our senses to feel connected and embodied. Taste, smell, hearing, sight, and touch are often taken for granted in our daily lives. By intentionally bringing awareness to our senses, we can bring ourselves back into self-connection through presence.

We can connect to ourselves more fully by being present to our outer sensory world. Presence is as simple as pausing to listen deeply, to truly see what is before you, to breathe in the aromas around you, or to savor the taste of the food you are eating. Each time we pause and bring awareness to our senses, we are deepening our contact with presence. Each time we remember to experience something through our senses we are also connected to what is here, now. This is important. This is an act of returning and remembering yourself that will help your inner journey.

Cultivating Inner Connection

Humans are wired for connection. It's through connection to self, family, tribe, and nature that our ancestors survived. As we have evolved into this modern era, we have lost this thread of connection and it impacts us acutely. Our sense of disconnection manifests in our lives in different ways such as a sense of deficiency, under-nourishment, isolation, despair, loneliness, frustration, darkness, numbness, etc.

We miss connection and we feel its absence within us as a longing, but we don't know how to satisfy that longing and are unable to connect with ourselves, others, nature, the divine, or an inner sense of aliveness. To feel or admit to any of these feelings is painful and we tend to suppress them.

As we will explore in the next chapters, what is suppressed remains unchanged and manifests as tense energy within us. When we suppress our painful sense of being disconnected, the feeling continues to resonate in the body, and it manifests in the negative feelings and thoughts listed above. As these feelings and thoughts stew beneath the surface of our lives, they reinforce our sense of disconnection even more. This is a cycle, circular, spiraling within. While it may feel like a never-ending cycle at times, rest assured it is not.

Our sense of disconnection is not dependent on whether we have people in our lives. People often feel lonelier in a crowd. Relationships can sometimes highlight our sense of disconnection rather than alleviate it. We long for connection and seek it outside of ourselves as a way of avoiding our pain, but the pain continues when we do not feel met or seen in our interactions.

As we began this journey together, I proposed that the two guideposts of integration were developing a sense of centeredness and connection.

One of the issues that comes up often in my integration sessions with clients is a renewed and reawakened sense of disconnection on all levels. It's like the plug gets pulled and the sense of connection felt during ceremony dissipates over time, and this creates a deep sense of anguish. No matter what the medicine opens for us —the feeling of being one with all life, the sense of being seen and heard by fellow travelers, or a sense of belonging to a tribe that is experienced during a medicine retreat—when we step back into our ordinary lives, we want to maintain this sense of belonging but often it feels elusory. "How do I bring back my sense of connection?" is a common integration question and a big dive into the mystery of being a human during this time.

We have all experienced being born and although we don't consciously remember that experience, it resides within us in our unconscious minds. We came from our mother's womb where we were held in a warm liquid pool, and our needs were met through a natural flow of energy and sustenance at our navel. When we were born, we experienced our first disconnect: we were suddenly shifted into breathing, crying little beings and our umbilical cord was cut. Imagine the shock of this experience. We hold this first sense of painful disconnect in our very bodies.

We were completely dependent on our caregivers for the first years of our lives. Our sense of needing connection was rooted in our survival instincts. These instincts are prioritized by our bodies' energy system above all else. We adapted our behaviors to ensure this connection.

From the beginning of our lives, our sense of connection is nurtured when we are held, comforted, and fed by our caregivers. In traditional Indigenous cultures this is a natural part of the baby's life. The baby is always held, and I have heard it is said that "The baby never touches the floor." There are aunties, uncles, grandmoms, grandpas, siblings and cousins who all take part in supporting the mother and baby in such a way that the sense of connection is firmly established and nourished within the baby.

In our Western culture we don't have this anymore. In most cases, parents are required to be multitaskers. They work outside of the home. They have been conditioned that it's better to let the baby cry at night so that it learns to adapt. Holding and comforting have been described as spoiling and indulging. Mothers are taught to feed the baby on a schedule rather than when the baby is hungry, and thus the baby cries because their needs are not being met. When this happens the baby, who is longing for secure connection, ends up feeling unwanted, unimportant, and disconnected.

The baby then grows up and continues to seek to reconnect by plugging its umbilical cord into other people or behaviors, substituting, trying to fill the gap; what's really happening is the person is trying to alleviate the deep pain of this early disconnection. The problem is the pain of disconnection is an internal wound, and it can't be healed through relating to others or substituting with outer stimuli until it is healed within by connecting with ourselves.

"The body is the shore on the ocean of being."
– Ancient Sufi saying

Remembering the Felt Sense

Indeed, connecting to self is an important aspect of the integration journey. We started with bringing awareness and attention to our five senses. Let's deepen now with another layer of self-connection: the *felt sense*. The idea of felt sense was developed by Eugene Gendlin in the 1960s as he studied what made therapy most effective. Gendlin noticed that people who made real progress in therapy had a certain inner awareness, a vague, bodily feeling that wasn't quite an emotion or a thought, but a meaningful sense of something inside. He called this the felt sense. Gendlin then developed a simple (but not easy) method to connect with this inner sense, with the understanding that connection happens when we pause, turn inward, and listen to the body.[6]

The felt sense is the actual sensation in the body. Our bodies are finely wrought instruments that are constantly regulating based on both our inner and outer environments. Every moment, our bodies are responding to our

6 Gendlin, Eugene T. *Focusing*. Revised edition. New York: Bantam Books, 1996.

surroundings. This happens so automatically that we are not aware of it. To understand the felt sense, we must tune into our bodily sensations. The felt sense is the first layer of our ability to experience our lives authentically. It informs and influences our emotional reactions and thinking minds. Through it we experience our own authentic self-connection.

"A felt sense is not a mental experience but a physical one. Physical. A bodily awareness of a situation or person or event. An internal aura that encompasses everything you feel and know about the given subject at a given time—encompasses it and communicates it to you all at once rather than detail by detail. Think of it as a taste, if you like, or a great musical chord that makes you feel a powerful impact, a big round unclear feeling. A felt sense doesn't come to you in the form of thoughts or words or other separate units, but as a single (though often puzzling and very complex) bodily feeling."

—Eugene Gendlin

The felt sense is a doorway to authentic connection with self and others. For many of us it has become illusory, because we have forgotten the language of the body and are conditioned to turn our conscious awareness to our thinking mind and its interpretation of outer cues. Our felt sense is a doorway to access and heal past trauma, and it connects us to our intuition and deeper eternal wisdom. Unfortunately, most of us disconnect from bodily awareness at an early age because when our natural instinctual needs are not met, we end up losing access to our felt sense. Our minds become the dominate lens through which we experience this world and our lives.

The felt sense informs us consciously and unconsciously all the time. Learning to tap into this wisdom of the body through the felt sense is the path to deeper self-connection and presence. The journey to self is an inner journey, and one we often miss because we seek understanding from outside of ourselves. Our felt sense is an invaluable tool on the inner journey of returning to self-trust and wholeness.

Cultivating your felt sense can help you to integrate your ceremony. Integration is not a puzzle for the mind to figure out; it is a full-body experience. In terms of integration, there are many benefits to connecting to the felt sense, including: recognizing and understanding the language of your body in order to receive the messages it's sending, cultivating a heightened sensitivity and deepening of self-attunement and intuition, becoming more grounded and at home in your body by increasing presence. It is a key to integration.

We practice the felt sense by paying attention to the sensations in our bodies. It takes practice and intention, especially at first. What are the sensations in the body? They are not emotions or feelings or perceptions, but the physical experience of the body itself. Sensations might include:

- Body temperature: warm, hot, burning, cool, cold, clammy, chills, icy (Example: I feel my face grow hot as I speak.)
- Pressure: even, uneven, supportive, heavy (Example: my chest feels heavy.)
- Tension: solid, dense, warm, cold, protective, constricting, angry, sad, loose, tight (Example: my stomach feels like it has a knot in it.)
- Pain: ache, sharp, twinge, slight, stabbing (Example: I feel a twinge in my left wrist.)
- Tingling: pricks, vibration, tickling, numb (Example: my hands are tingling.)
- Itch: mild itch, angry itch, irritating itch, subtle itch, small itch, large area of itching (Example: I feel a burning itch in my lower legs during meditation.)
- Weight: light, heavy (Example: my body feels heavy; I feel lighthearted.)
- Color: (Example: I feel a red haze inside; my heart is blue.)

My first experience of the felt sense was during a craniosacral session many years ago with a woman that I deeply admired and respected, Arpita. I felt a bit intimidated by her and so was quite nervous going into the session. I wasn't sure what to expect as a fledging seeker and so when she asked me to drop into my body it was quite disconcerting. My mind had prepared many narratives that I thought I needed to explore. I found a fluttering sensation and hot pressure in my chest. After describing this to her and staying with it she asked me the simple question: "What do I need?" My felt sense answered almost immediately: I need safety. I needed to feel safe. I realized this need was pervasive in my life and not about the immediate session. Together we found a posture with my hands gently holding my face that I could breathe into to feel safe and I continue to use this posture and breathe into it whenever these sensations arise. This was and still is a powerful tool in my toolkit, and antidote to the narratives of my mind, which take me out of presence.

Self-Exploration Exercise: Felt Sense

This simple practice helps you tune into the subtle, bodily awareness known as the felt sense. It may feel like a vague, internal something that is not quite a thought or an emotion, but a whole-body sense of a situation or feeling, without words.[7]

Step 1. Settle and Pause

Find a quiet space. Sit comfortably and allow yourself a few moments to slow down. Let your attention turn inward. You don't need to fix anything, just notice what's there.

Step 2. Gently Ask

Bring to mind a situation that is present in your life, something that feels meaningful but not overwhelming. For instance, maybe

---

7 Please note: It is important for people who have experienced severe trauma to get support in remembering the felt sense if feeling in the body is at all triggering. When we start to relearn the language of the body experiences, emotions, and memories may surface to be released and healed and support is key.

you don't want to go to work, or you had a rough interaction with a loved one. Now, ask yourself:

"How does this feel in my body right now?"

Don't rush to answer. Wait for a sensation to form in your body. If unclear, just continue to listen inward. No pressure.

Step 3. Notice What Comes

Pay attention to the vague physical feeling that arises. It might be in your chest, stomach, throat or somewhere else. It might feel like tightness, pressure, fluttering, etc.

Step 4. Describe It Gently

Try to find a few words, an image, or a metaphor for the feeling. Maybe it's like a tight ball, a cloud, a sinking stone, or a buzzing. Stay with it, curiously and kindly.

Step 5. Listen

See if the felt sense shifts a little as you pay attention. You're not analyzing, you're listening. You might notice a small release, a change in breath, or a new insight. That's the body's way of moving forward.

This process may feel too subtle at first, but with practice it can become a powerful way to access and strengthen your sense of connection to yourself.

Another way to connect to your felt sense is to practice asking yourself throughout the day, "How am I doing?" then stop for a few minutes and feel into the body, noticing any sensations. Another cue: whenever anyone asks you how you are, instead of automatically answering, "Fine," take a few seconds and see what the body might share through the felt sense before answering.

How many times has someone asked you, "How are you?" and you have replied, "Oh, I'm fine," without giving it a thought? This is what we do to our own selves in our own bodies. We don't inhabit our bodies, and our lives are less rich, less vibrant, less connected as a result. The felt sense is the thread with which we weave the ceremony of our lives. If we are out of touch with this sense of self, how can we heal what our body remembers, how can we be present, how can we be embodied?

Journal Reflection Prompts: Felt Sense

After experimenting with your felt sense in the present, journal about the sensations you were able to uncover. If it feels right, also see if you can remember the sensations of your body during ceremony. Did you feel hot, cold, heavy, light, itchy, or was there pain? Journal about this felt sense and explore what you think the medicine was up to without trying to interpret it as good or bad.

Other Ways to Connect to Self Through the Body

Dr. Peter Levine, founder of Somatic Experiencing, has spent decades exploring how trauma is held in the body and how it can be gently released. His work shows that trauma is not just a psychological experience, but a physiological one stored in the nervous system as unresolved energy. Healing begins when we reconnect with the body and allow that energy to safely move.

To support this process, Levine developed simple, accessible tools that help people return to a sense of safety and presence. Two of these, tapping and the showerhead technique, offer powerful ways to reconnect with the body and with oneself during integration.[8]

Self-Exploration Exercise: Tapping and the Showerhead Techniques

Tapping involves gently and rhythmically patting different areas of the body, such as the arms, chest, or legs. This tactile engagement helps bring

---

8 Levine, Peter A. *Waking the Tiger: Healing Trauma*. Berkeley, CA: North Atlantic Books, 1997, page 63.

awareness back into the body, reestablish physical boundaries, and regulate overwhelming sensations. It's particularly helpful when someone feels disconnected, dissociated, or emotionally shut down. Tapping provides a direct, physical reminder that *you are here, and your body is with you*.

Levine's shower head technique is a gentle method to support nervous system regulation. By using a handheld shower head with cool or warm water set to a pulsing or massaging spray, one can slowly guide the water over different parts of the body. While doing this we name the body parts, "this is my arm, this is my leg, etc., I welcome you back." This exercise re-establishes connection with our bodies. As the warm pulses make contact, attention is directed inward to notice sensations: such as tingling, softening, or warmth, without forcing anything to happen. This simple yet effective practice can help discharge stored tension, awaken body awareness, and facilitate a sense of safety and grounding, especially during integration work.

Both practices are gentle pathways back to self-connection. Integration requires a sense of inner wholeness, and these techniques help rebuild trust in the body and reestablish a sense of being home inside oneself, embodied.

When we are embodied (connected to our bodies) we can then bring awareness to our inner landscape. When we are disconnected from our bodies, we are also disconnected from our inner wisdom and authentic selves.

"The body will never misguide you, you can trust it, and you can trust it absolutely."

-Osho

Self-connection starts with connection to the body. These simple exercises, practiced consistently over time, can support what should be a natural part of being alive but instead have become illusory for many of us.

The Healing Power of Connection to Others

While much of the integration process is an inward journey, the presence of trusted friends, companions, or teachers can act as a powerful mirror and grounding force. Sharing space with those who have walked a similar path, be it a fellow ceremony attendee, a close friend, or a supportive integration group, can offer reassurance that we are not alone in our experience. After a sacred plant ceremony, presence, empathy, and deep listening can provide the reflection we need to feel seen and held.

A trusted friend or spiritual ally can offer gentle support without trying to interpret or fix our process. Simply having someone witness our unfolding can be deeply regulating for the nervous system and affirming for the psyche. These safe containers of relationship allow us to speak our truth, voice our confusion, and share our joy or deep gratitude.

Self-Exploration Exercise: Intentional Sharing

One way to approach building community and connection is to create a sharing ritual. This can be done in a dyad of two or a small group. Every person has a designated amount of time to share. I recommend keeping these sharing times short, ten minutes maximum. The speaker says whatever comes to the surface. The listeners simply provide an abiding presence, with no response, no insertion, no interpretation, or advice. When an individual's time ends, everyone gives thanks. It's important that no one gives feedback after the sharing unless specifically asked to do so and that each sharing is held as sacred and confidential. Creating a container for sharing to keep it succinct and manageable is key. Presence is required and if one person starts to ramble on unchecked the attunement of the group dissipates.

If you're feeling disconnected, finding group integration circles or community spaces can offer the support of shared wisdom and camaraderie. Hearing others articulate their challenges and realizations often brings clarity to our own. In these spaces, we remember that we are not alone. Listening to others can increase self-understanding and reinforce the sacredness of the path we are on. In my work I have learned that these integration circles can be incredibly healing. As we go around the circle taking turns, people often share that words already spoken by others resonate deeply with their own experience, that others are articulating a common theme or shared understanding from the ceremony.

Of course, this type of outer connection and support is not a replacement for the inner journey. However, feeling the support and empathy of fellow travelers can be incredibly healing. When rooted in authenticity, respect, and presence, our relationships can become part of the integration path itself. They help weave our understandings, our fears, our longing back into the fabric of our three-dimensional human life, grounding us in shared meaning and mutual support.

Finally, finding a trusted and attuned therapist or integration coach *who has an understanding/experience* of sacred plant medicine can be the key to integration The sense of being held in the abiding presence of being heard, seen, understood and supported can heal us deeply. This is what we needed in our early years and experiencing it in the present can relax and relieve that sense of not being held, understood, or attuned to here and now.

When we are embodied and connected to self this creates the foundation to have genuine connection with others and reawakens the felt sense of being connected to all.

Chapter Six: Creating Healthy Boundaries

> *"Daring to set boundaries is about having the courage to love ourselves. Even when we risk disappointing others."*
>
> —Brene Brown

Another important aspect of connection is the ability to *disconnect* when appropriate. Healthy boundaries are also important for your integration process. As we have explored, your plant medicine experience needs space to unfold and take root. You might feel more open and extremely sensitive after your experience. While this openness can be transformative, it also leaves a person more vulnerable in the days and weeks that follow. Boundaries, both internal (like emotional limits and self-care practices) and external (like choosing who to share with and setting time for solitude), help create a safe container for integration. They protect the unfolding, allow space for the medicine's vibration to continue, and prevent overwhelm. Healthy boundaries are another key to integration.

Setting healthy boundaries is a vital part of emotional well-being, self-awareness, and self-care, especially in the vulnerable and transformative space of plant medicine integration. After a plant medicine journey, you may feel more open, sensitive, or emotionally raw. Your usual filters and defenses may be temporarily lowered, which can create space for profound understanding but also a need for protection and grounding. Boundaries help you hold and honor what's been revealed, allowing healing to deepen rather than unravel.

The first step in setting boundaries is listening to your body and inner sense of what feels safe, nourishing, or overwhelming. You might notice that you need more rest, quiet time, or solitude than usual. Or you may find that certain conversations, environments, or people feel too stimulating and out of sync with your integration. These signals are important. Ask yourself: what do I need right now to feel supported in this integration? What feels like it's too much? Boundaries are how you give these needs real attention in your life.

During integration, boundaries might look like limiting social interactions, choosing carefully who you share your experience with, or taking space from digital input or intense environments. Communicate clearly and kindly, even if simply saying, "I'm processing a lot right now and need some quiet time," or "I'm not ready to talk about my experience yet." You don't have to justify your boundaries; honoring your process is reason enough.

Boundaries are not about shutting others out, they're about staying connected to yourself. In the context of plant medicine integration, they help protect the vibration that is continuing to resonate in your being from the ceremony that you worked so hard to participate in. Without boundaries, it's easy to slip back into old patterns, distractions, or relationships that don't support your integration. With boundaries, you give your integration the time, space, and respect it needs.

Journal Reflection Prompts: Boundaries

When is it easy and when is it difficult to set boundaries? While working with this prompt try to focus on your body sensations. What does your body feel like when it is easy to set a boundary? What happens in your body when setting a healthy boundary is difficult? Not sure? Remember a recent specific instance and then observe your body sensations and write them down.

Self-Exploration Exercise: Boundaries – The Body Speaks

Many years ago, in another version of myself just after law school, I took a weeklong trial advocacy training to hone my litigation skills. The one lesson that has stuck with me from this rather intense and intimidating week was a simple hand gesture to control an adverse witness. We were taught to hold our arm out straight, palm facing toward the witness, no words needed. The universal signal for stop. This signal is visceral, real and rooted in the moment. Practice this gesture. Stand firmly and hold your arm out palm facing up. Sense how it feels within your being. Use it as a tool for your own boundary setting. It's a powerful embodiment of *No, Stop,* without words, processing, or explanation required. You can use this for yourself. Whenever you feel a yes coming that intuitively doesn't align to support your healthy boundaries just take the posture and breathe into it. Stop. I don't mean for you to use this posture physically with your loved ones, unless it's necessary, but in practicing it, feel the energy that it evokes within you and then call on that energy as needed.

Creating healthy boundaries allows our bodies to relax and feel safe thereby calming our nervous systems. When our nervous systems are calm our minds are calm, and our emotions are more balanced.

Chapter Seven:

The Nervous System as Sacred Ally

At the heart of our ability to truly integrate is the state of our nervous system. As we are exploring, integration is deeply physiological. To support integration, the body must feel safe.

The nervous system, particularly the autonomic branch, governs how we respond to stress, rest, and connection. It's the invisible river within carrying our whole beings' primal messages of safety or threat. During ceremony, this system may be profoundly activated, whether by awe, fear, grief, release, or bliss. Afterward, the work of integration cannot take place without having our nervous systems online to support our efforts. Without this, integration can feel overwhelming or fragmented.

Understanding Nervous System Regulation

Nervous system regulation is the process of guiding ourselves back into a state of balance after activation. Stephen W. Porges, PhD, has written a book called *The Pocket Guide to the Polyvagal Theory: The Transformative Power of Feeling Safe* and created an accessible framework for understanding the nervous system. We studied this during my advanced training in trauma informed inquiry, and I found it extremely helpful both for my own nervous system regulation and for the clients I support in my integration sessions. In the language of polyvagal theory, we shift between the sympathetic (fight/flight), dorsal vagal (shutdown/freeze), and ventral vagal (connection/safety) states.[9] Each state expresses itself through subtle shifts in breath, heart rate, posture, voice, and mood. Integration is most supported when we can access the ventral state, where presence, receptivity, and healing unfold.

Tracking these changing states within can be very challenging, because as Peter Levine teaches in his book *Waking the Tiger*, they are hard wired in our DNA for our very survival. For the most part, we don't choose to enter sympathetic or shutdown state, it just happens. Levine teaches that trauma is not the activating or traumatic event itself, but the inability to complete the process of moving *through* the event that creates the actual trauma. Unlike animals in the wild, who instinctively shake, tremble, or run to release the excess energy of a threat, humans often suppress these natural responses due to social conditioning or fear. As a result, the energy of activation remains trapped in the nervous system, contributing to patterns of chronic tension, anxiety, or trauma.

Make attuning to your nervous system part of your integration journey. When we learn to track our sensations and nervous system states through our felt sense, we can then apply simple tools to self-soothe or re-engage our nervous systems, thereby allowing us to become active participants in our healing. We become fluent in our body's signals, and in doing so, we learn to listen more deeply and take responsibility for the state of our nervous systems.

In the simplest of terms, it's important to note if your nervous system is in a state of flight, fight, shutdown or freeze so that you can then take care to complete the energy movement that your nervous system needs. If, for example, you are in an argument with your partner and you feel yourself going into freeze (unresponsive, unable to access your emotions or feel your heart) ask to take a break from the conversation to allow yourself space to address this response.

---

9 Porges, Stephen W. *The Pocket Guide to the Polyvagal Theory: The Transformative Power of Feeling Safe*. New York: Norton Professional Books, 2017.

Listening To the Language of the Nervous System

Accessing the state of your nervous system begins with noticing the body's cues, rhythms, and sensations. Each state expresses itself through subtle shifts in breath, heart rate, posture, voice, and mood. To assess your state, begin by asking: am I feeling connected, alert, and open? Am I tense, agitated, numb, or disconnected? If you feel warm, engaged, and present, you're likely in ventral vagal state of regulation, where healing and integration are possible. If you feel keyed-up, anxious, or irritable, that's your sympathetic system activating. If you feel heavy, foggy, or collapsed, you may be in a dorsal vagal state. These aren't bad or wrong states of being, they are your body's adaptive responses to keep you safe. The key is recognizing where you are without judgment.

My trauma training included somatic and nervous-system-based approaches inspired by Somatic Experiencing, which I've continued to explore in collaboration with colleagues in that field. This is beautiful, powerful work. Dr. Peter Levine emphasizes that healing trauma (and I'd add that supporting integration) involves tracking sensation and respecting the body's pacing. He teaches us to notice small shifts, like a sigh, a muscle releasing, or a new awareness in the body, as signs of regulation. You can practice this by pausing several times a day and checking in to see if you are drawn to move or be still. The key is to then follow your inner guide. If you sense your nervous system needs release by movement, move. If you sense your nervous system needs stillness, provide this and breathe into it. Just a few minutes of awareness is all it takes. If you feel like your nervous system needs attention, here are a few simple tools that can help bring your nervous system back into the ventral state.

Self-Exploration Exercise: Simple Tools for Nervous System Support

Both Porges and Levine teach simple tools for nervous system regulation.

1. Orienting
   Gently turn your head and look around your space. Let your

eyes land on objects, colors, or shapes. Name what you see aloud or silently. This simple act tells the body that it is safe.

2. Grounding Touch
   Place one hand on your chest and the other on your belly. Feel the warmth and pressure. You can add slow breathing, extending your exhale to calm the system.

3. Weighted Blanket or Compression
   Use a blanket or even your own hands to apply gentle pressure to your shoulders, thighs, or back. This helps the body feel contained and held.

4. Humming or Vagal Toning
   Humming, chanting, or even singing softly stimulates the vagus nerve, which helps activate the parasympathetic (rest-and-digest) response.

5. Cold Water or Sensory Reset
   Splash cold water on your face, hold a cool object, or take a brisk walk. Engaging the senses can reset over-activation.

6. Rhythmic Movement
   Sway side to side or gently rock yourself with your arms crossed and resting on opposite arms in a being-held gesture. The body responds to swaying, rhythm and holding as soothing and familiar.

7. Shaking
   Stand up and shake your body. Start with the hands and arms and then allow the whole body to move freely, shaking for several minutes. Let your body move in support of the shaking and bonus points if you raise your arms above your shoulders as you shake at times. Imagine your body becoming liquid, loose, releasing energies.

By learning to listen inwardly with curiosity rather than control, and then actually following though and giving your body what it needs, your nervous system can become a sacred ally to your integration process and life.

Your body is a sensitive, intelligent companion on your integration journey. A regulated nervous system creates the soil for your integration to take root and grow. When we practice self-regulation, we take responsibility for the state of our being.

In this way, integration becomes less about effort and more about attunement. You don't have to fix or figure it all out. Instead, learn to return to yourself repeatedly, with breath, with stillness, with touch, and let your nervous system show you the path of trust and safety.

Explore Active Meditation: Kundalini Meditation to Restore Calm

Osho's Kundalini Meditation is an hour-long active meditation that can completely reset your nervous system. I have been leading kundalini meditation once a week for the last twenty-plus years and I highly recommend it as a wonderful way to transition from your busy day to a calmer ventral state for your evening. Our daily lives are stressful and packed with frenetic energies. People are stressed, rushed, and tired. Thus, to implement a practice that allows you to release whatever energies you have absorbed or engaged with during the day as a conscious choice can be empowering and very supportive of your nervous system regulation, your overall health, and your integration journey. Plus, it's fun.

Kundalini is another name for your life-force energy that we will explore at great length in the following chapters. For now, think of it as energy stored at the base of your spine that moves, or very much wants to move, up through your chakra system. If this energy is blocked and doesn't flow, our life force is also stuck, we are not able to be totally present in our life, and we lack vitality and feel dull. Our body, mind and spirit are affected in all kinds of ways by our blocked energy, none of them helpful or healthful. We want our energy to move.

So how does it work? Kundalini Meditation is done in four 15-minute stages. The first stage is shaking the body with eyes closed. You want to be loose and allow the body to shake rather than doing the shaking. If done with total commitment, over time you will start to feel the energy rising up the spine. The more you allow your body to move on its own, rather than moving it, the more powerful the effect.

> *"When I say shaking, I mean your solidity, your rock-like being should shake to the foundations so that it becomes liquid, fluid, melts, flows. And when the rock like being becomes liquid, your body will follow. Then there is no shaker, only shaking. Then nobody is doing it, it is simply happening. Then the doer is not."*
>
> —Osho

The second stage is dancing, and you again allow your body to move as it feels to without mindful effort but in totality. This is a stage of mini celebration; allowing the eyes to close and the body to move freely supported by beautiful music is a gift to self.

The third stage is sitting and simply witnessing within. Here, having moved our energy with totality we are invited to sit in stillness and meditation. Following release and movement, this sitting meditation feels natural and easeful, rather than awkward and difficult.

The fourth stage is relaxation, where we lay down on our backs in a *savasana* posture and allow our bodies to completely let go.

The music to this Osho Kundalini Meditation can be found on streaming platforms. If an hour feels too long you can also just do five minutes of each stage as a mini-Kundalini, for a total of twenty minutes. Why not?

Chapter Eight:

Resistance, All That You Are Holding Inside

"Your task is not to seek for love, but merely to seek and find all the barriers within yourself that you have built against it."

—Rumi

Resistance often appears during integration as a pulling away from our processes and ceremony homework. It might show up as avoidance, distraction, over-analysis, emotional numbness, or even a sudden surge of doubt about our entire experience. After a plant medicine ceremony, where understandings may have been bestowed upon us in vivid, heart-opening clarity, resistance can feel confusing or frustrating. A common narrative that comes up in my integration sessions is: Why am I turning away from something I know will help me, support me, and make me feel better?

Resistance is not the enemy. It protects us from moving too fast, too deep, or too far beyond what feels safe to the nervous system. In this sense, it is a form of intelligence. However, when left unexplored, resistance can also become a barrier that prevents integration from taking root. The medicine may have revealed a new way of being, but the old patterns that are familiar and comforting want to pull us back into unconscious habits that self-soothe and self-protect.

Working with resistance means gently bringing awareness to where we push away the very understandings we longed to receive. It requires patience, humility, and compassion. Rather than fighting resistance, we can become curious by asking: What is this part of me afraid will happen if I continue to explore? Often, underneath resistance is pain, fear, or our core wounds feeling exposed and vulnerable. It's important to understand that resistance is energetically fueled by all the forces we are holding at bay within us. By naming and witnessing this, we loosen their grip and allow a deeper conversation to emerge.

During our integration journey, resistance is a signal. It invites us to slow down, breathe into discomfort, and reconnect with our intention. When we can hold resistance with presence rather than judgment, it transforms from an obstacle into a doorway.

Consider thinking of your resistance as a powerful energy, a dynamic force that is dwelling in your personal unconscious mind to protect you. Not only that, it is also an energetic force that is patterned in the unconscious minds of your family, friends, and other familiars, who are not seeking change and maybe don't want to see you change. Further, this energy force is deeply connected to and swirling in the collective unconscious of our culture whose influences are felt in almost all aspects of our lives. By understanding that your resistance is a powerful energy force that dwells within and without your being, originally created to keep you safe and alive, perhaps you can drop any negative messaging about resistance and greet it with humor and compassion.

When we judge our resistance as a personal failure and then try to dismiss or discard it because we want to get rid of it, we actually reinforce it. In essence, by resisting our resistance, we are reinforcing its power over us. Again, we see the theme of circularity and cycles in integration. We do not want to be in opposition to the tremendous energy force within us that is resistance.

Accepting our resistance and giving it the deep respect that it deserves takes courage and honesty. If you feel resistance to any part of your integration journey, whether it's taking space in nature, feeling emotions that are coming up, having an intuitive understanding and ignoring it, try to just bring awareness to the resistance without judging it. Whether you push through the resistance and get out in nature or end up not going on the hike, if you can acknowledge that the resistance is there and a part of the process without judging it, you will have a much easier time working with it. Respect it. Honor it. Its job is to keep you safe, so thank it.

"Whether we like it or not, change comes, and the greater the resistance, the greater the pain. Buddhism perceives the beauty of change, for life is like music in this: if any note or phrase is held for longer than its appointed time, the melody is lost."

—Alan Watts

Journal Reflection Prompts: Explore Resistance

How do I experience resistance right now in my integration process?

Using the felt sense, where do I feel resistance in my body? What might it be trying to tell me?

What would happen if I allowed myself to soften by greeting this resistance with compassion and humor?

These prompts can help bring compassionate awareness to the natural push-pull of resistance and help you befriend this frustrating companion we all share.

Part Two
Welcoming Our Ceremony Guests

Now that we've created a safe container for our integration we can move into exploring our inner world so that we can deepen our understanding of the various aspects at play in this process. Our energetic system, our bodies, our navel center, our mind, viewed through several lenses, multifaceted and multilayered, and our emotional center are all the guests we are greeting and welcoming to our circle. We want to greet each guest with presence, attunement, compassion, and humor.

Chapter Nine:

Everything Is Comprised of Energy, Including Us

"Everything is energy and that is all there is to it. Match the frequency of the reality you want and you cannot help but get that reality. It can be no other way. This is not philosophy. This is physics."

—Albert Einstein

Our first ceremony guest that we greet and begin to get to know is our energy system. Integration is when our inner energy is able to move naturally and when our outer energy matches this in frequency and vibration.

Often on sacred plant journeys, we experience energy in a new way, through colors, visions, and vibrations. During ceremony, as we shift consciousness, our senses are amplified and our sensitivity increases, and we access unfamiliar energy patterns that are incredible, blissful, bewildering, and at times scary.

So, let's start here with energy. What the ancient wisdom keepers have known for millennia, has now been confirmed by quantum physics: everything is energy. In our day-to-day reality, we are accustomed to experiencing energy through our five senses. Depending on our awareness and sensitivity, our bodies respond to the energy we are living in and interpret our experiences based on these sensory perceptions. We see the first wildflowers of spring peeking out. We smell the lilac blossoms. We taste the ginger tea we are sipping. We feel the warmth of the cup as we hold it in our hands. These visceral experiences make up our day-to-day world and we completely take them for granted, as we explored in the previous chapter. This is the plane of existence that we live in on Mother Earth, Pachamama: tactile, familiar, and for most of us (most of the time) three-dimensional.

Many of us are aware of other energies that are not tactile, such as a sense of intuition that arises within us: that light bulb moment of knowing. This is another form of energy that is also familiar.

When we journey with plant medicines, we experience an expanded perception of energy that we might see without seeing, hear without sound, and feel without touch. As we expand our consciousness, we might see bright colors and lights in amazing patterns, images of nature or celestial beings, incredible, vibrant, and vibrational imagery. We might hear music or voices or receive messages that seem real to us but that no one else hears.

One way of understanding these energies is that the patterns and colors we see or sounds we hear are the vibration—the song and dance—of the plant energy. This vibration is repeated and invited by the vibration of the music that accompanies the ceremony. The traditional icaros of the grandmother medicine, the hypnotic water drum and rattle of the peyote medicine, the astonishing and powerful Australian Aboriginal digeridoo, the vibration of the Tibetan bowls and gongs, these are all the vibration of the healing energy of the universe itself. As such, they are aligned and directed by existence and, in this context of ceremony, by the sacred plant medicine. The colors and patterns are created by the vibrational matrix of the plant energy.

One of the most healing aspects for many who journey is sensing and experiencing the vibration and the visions that accompany these medicines. This vibration is energy beyond our normal sensory world. We experience it and we are healed through it, and we are left wondering about it: Is it real? Is it made up in the mind? It is powerful and magical and mysterious and not tangible in our day-to-day, three-dimensional worlds? There is an understanding that while each individual journey is different, these patterns and vibrations are universally experienced. Witness the repetition in the paintings, arts, and crafts of the Indigenous Wisdom Keepers throughout the world; the same patterns are repeated throughout because they all come from the same universal source: truth.

This energy is not limited to the realms of altered states of consciousness. After my first visit down to South America for my first dieta, I experienced some confusion as to whether plant medicine was in contradiction to my traditional Eastern meditation path. Three weeks after returning from Peru, I found myself in Dharamsala, India where I had gone to study Gurdjieff Sacred Movement (an entirely different path into the unknowable within and without) and as I landed there before the group began, I was wandering through the Tibetan settlement and was deeply touched by the patterns of their Thangka paintings[10] and the vibration of the sacred mantras that reverberated through the streets of the tiny village. One day as I was meandering through, I experienced a deep breakthrough: truth is universal. The vibration of the plant medicine of the Amazon Rainforest is the same vibration I was experiencing here, now, in Dharamsala. The patterns in the Thangka paintings were the same patterns depicted in South American tapestries and the mantras carried the same healing sound vibration. I was so struck by this realization that I was moved to tears. It felt like such a gift to realize that my path might vary but the destination was the same. Truth is one and its vibration is universal, held by the wisdom keepers.

Everything is energy. We too are made up of energy. Our bodies, our cells, our DNA are all just matter, matter that is made up of energy patterns. We are familiar with the energy in our bodies mainly in terms of the way we feel and how we fuel our systems. We know that we need to eat and drink to function. We know if we are low on energy or feeling energized as a matter of course in our daily life. For instance, coffee gives our energy a boost. We are aware that the chemical energy that comprises our diet is digested and then transformed into other forms of energy, such as kinetic energy for movement and electrical energy for nerve impulses.

But there is another way of understanding energy within the human framework and this matters in terms of integration. When we have an experience of visions and vibrations, we might also sense that they are not separate from us and our world. Just because we have only experienced them through the altered state of consciousness caused by the plant medicine does

---

10 Tibetan thangka paintings are sacred scroll paintings used as meditation aids and teaching tools. Their intricate patterns often depict mandalas, cosmological maps, and symbolic motifs that represent stages of the spiritual path and the structure of the universe.

not mean that they are not a part of the day-to-day world, it simply means that we are not sensitive enough to perceive them.

Another way to understand these concepts is to trust that the vibrations and visions are an experience of truth: this truth being that everything is connected, everything is one. We will revisit this concept in depth later in this integration journey, but for now consider and be curious about the following: everything is energy; there is one energy; and you are connected to that energy always, even on this plane. The language of oneness is a language long forgotten, a sensitivity lost.

Your integration journey is a journey to remember and reconnect to this energy on the three-dimensional plane. It is an inner journey that requires a deeper dive into your being. You won't find it outside of yourself. It is within.

Medicine moves energy within. Part of the healing that occurs when we imbibe sacred plant medicine is happening on the level of energy. Ayahuasca works with us energetically; she likes to shake things up, stir the pot, scrape the burnt charred edges of our inner beings that we didn't even know needed attention and our energy moves in response. Our energy shifts not necessarily towards what we want, but with what we need. This process can be so primal, forceful, awkward, unladylike if you will, with loud purging, groans, releasing on the toilet. Our bodies purge and shake and sweat and shiver and twitch. This is the medicine finding and moving stuck energy. This can be terrifying in the moment, but it is how we heal.

Before we move on, consider this: when we are in a state of disintegration we are either in a state of stuck or racing energy. Our life force energy is not in a natural flow. This directly impacts our nervous systems. If our energy is racing ahead of us, we experience anxiety; our natural flight response has kicked in and instead of running we try to tamp it down or ignore it, and so we become more anxious. If our energy is stuck in the past, we experience a depressed state: no vitality, creativity, or joy. The more we ignore the state the more we reinforce it. Circular. This creates a powerful tension within our beings that ultimately leads to disease. When our nervous systems are forced to fight the natural flow of life, which includes times of rest and times of productivity, we end up reinforcing our protections that no longer serve us, our adaptations that keep us safe but separate, our resistance. Denying our natural energy states is a way of saying no to life. We want to say yes to life, to feeling vital, creative, strong. And we *can*, if we can access the natural rhythm and flow of our life-force energy. When our energy flows, we are naturally integrated.

Chapter Ten:

Finding Energetic Harmony Within Through Elemental Balance

"Your body is not a thing. It is a happening. It is a pattern, a dance, of energy. It is the universe being you."

—Alan Watts

How can we work with our life-force energy? The idea that everything, including us, is just energy can feel vague. So, let's explore how Indigenous Wisdom Keepers have understood and categorized these energies, giving us a more grounded framework. Let's invite and welcome these guests into our integration ceremony.

The wisdom keepers of the world teach balance as an essential part of living in integrity—with our fellow humans, with Pachamama, and with all beings. On the sacred path of integration, finding balance is not about rigidity, but about fluidity. The integration process asks us to return to the inner harmony that plant medicine so often reminds us of with vivid clarity. While the external world pulls us in many directions, the journey of integration calls us inward. One way of understanding this inner journey is to explore the elemental forces that shape not only the natural world but also our internal landscape.

As I've shared, over the last decades I've been blessed to spend time with the wisdom keepers and healers of the Andes and the Amazon Rainforest of Peru. Years ago, a friend, teacher, and curandero generously taught me an ancient Andean song that I now sing in ceremony with permission. This beautiful song, in Quechua, is dedicated to the Inca Empire, *Tawantinsuyu*. It carries a distinct and playful rhythm, serving as a prayer that calls in the blessed ancestors, plantas maestras, wisdom keepers, animals, and spirits for guidance and support. It originates from the ancient spiritual traditions of the Andes and holds a vibration that feels alive in me when I sing it. For you, fellow traveler and reader, I share it here—*con permiso*.

The song begins by calling on the Four Sacred Directions: South (*qulla*), West (*kunti*), North (*chinchay*), and East (*anti*), invoking their protection and support. We then call in the center (*chawpin*). I was taught that the center is the heart, and to give it plenty of space in the song to ensure its strong presence in the ceremony. After honoring the directions, we call in the Four Sacred Elements from which all life is formed: Earth (*allpa*), Air (*wayra*), Water (*unu*), and Fire (*nina*).

After we have called in the Four Directions and Sacred Elements, the medicine, huachuma or ayahuasca, depending on the ceremony, guides us to invite sacred allies to support the work based on the needs of the participants. These allies are neither random nor accidental. They are invited to the ceremony through the wisdom of the medicine and its innate intelligence in the moment. Commonly called allies include the plantas maestras and maestros (the many master plants of the Andes and Amazon, each with its own personality and healing energy). Other allies include *Taita Inti* (Father Sun), *Mama Cocha* (the oceans), and *Mama Killa* (the moon), spirit beings such as the *Yacuruna* (healer spirits of the waters) and *Yacumama* (great serpent spirits); and sacred animals like *otorongo* (the jaguar) and *picaflor* (the hummingbird) and the tribes, the ancestors or the wisdom keepers who have stewarded these ceremonies for millennia. Each ally is called in with humility and intention, invited to lend their energetic presence to support the individual and collective journeys within the ceremonial space.

This order is important. First, we honor the directions: the source of origin. Then we call in the elements: the substance of creation. And only then do we invite the spirits to support our healing and learning. In doing so, we create a foundation for ceremony. This same foundation applies to your life, your healing, and the ceremony of integration.

This same curandero also taught me that the ancient Andean cross (*chakana*) represents the integration of the four sacred directions. Each direction corresponds with one of the sacred elements. Traditionally, these directions and their elements are considered living energies or deities to be honored, respected, and emulated. The universe is made of these energies, and so are we. The integration journey, then, is about recognizing and working with these elemental forces within ourselves, with the intention of returning to balance.

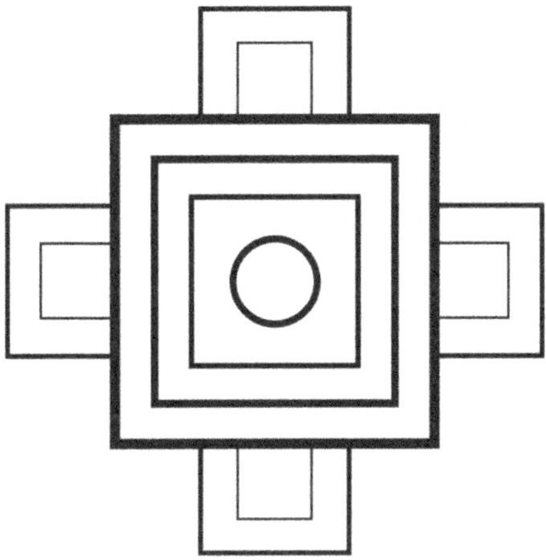

The four sacred directions and the four sacred elements of life are represented by the chakana. Chawpin is the center where they all connect. Symbolically, when the sacred elements are balanced and in harmony within us, we are then able to connect to and move from our own sacred center.

Our Inner Landscape Is Comprised of the Elements

"Breathing in, I see the element air in me. I see the clouds, snow, rain, and rivers in me. I see the atmosphere, wind, and forest in me, the mountains and oceans in me. I see the Earth in me."

—Thich Nhat Hanh

The chakana is representative of the Four Directions. Each direction then connects to an elemental energy that is universal to all things, including us.

Qulla: South, Pachamama

The key integration aspects of qulla are groundedness, support, and embodiment. Qulla is associated with our ancestors and represented by the serpent. The South corresponds to Pachamama. Pachamama is the animating energy of the physical Earth and is understood as a living, conscious being. She manifests not only in the physical world but also through the more subtle life energies, including the balance between our masculine and feminine aspects, our creative and destructive patterns, and the cycles of our lives. Pachamama is more than the planet we inhabit—she is the giver of life. She nurtures, feeds, and protects us. She sustains our lives in every way. Our bodies come from her and return to her, just as all of nature surrenders in this way. We are not merely made from her—we are a part of her. We *are* her.

Our human bodies also sustain and support us during our time on Earth. We are connected to Pachamama, and our physical forms are emanations of her energy. On the integration journey, the South can be seen as representing our physical body and material world. This is the first direction and element called in to support the ceremony of integration.

From an integration perspective, the South calls us to be present and connected to our bodies. On a practical level, this means tending to what sustains our lives and our day-to-day realities. On a more subtle level, it means reconnecting with the body as the place where healing unfolds, where release happens, and where our innate wisdom resides. When we approach this with gratitude for all we receive and bring awareness to reciprocity, our remembering, and our giving back, we move toward balance and harmony, both within and around us.

Kunti: West, Water

The next direction I call in the song is the West, kunti, which is associated with water. Within us, this element corresponds to our emotions, the unconscious, healing, and release; and is represented by the jaguar. In the Andean traditions, water is a symbol of divine femininity and the cyclical nature of life—birth, death, rebirth—and is closely linked to the moon. The West is synonymous with our emotional body. Most of us know that the moon regulates the tides of the oceans, but are we consciously aware of how the tides of our emotions influence our lives and thinking minds? Our emotions are fluid, and a helpful way to understand both conscious and unconscious feelings is to imagine them as the waters of the ocean—at times vast and deep, sometimes rising in waves, always shifting like the tides and crashing into the shore.

On our integration journey, our emotions, past and present, and those awakened in ceremony, are fertile ground for healing and self-knowledge. The unhealed emotions of our inner child long to be seen, acknowledged, and held. Our integration process can be seen as a journey of bringing aspects of our emotional body into conscious awareness. This means giving space to what was once suppressed, allowing our emotional waters to move freely and with presence. Understanding and feeling our emotions requires strength, courage, and trust—trust in our inner process as it unfolds in our everyday lives—just as we are asked to trust the process during ceremony. We will explore this more deeply in Chapter 16.

Chinchay: North, Air

After Kunti, in the song I then call in Chinchay, the North direction, whose key attributes include wind, clarity, communication, and vision. The North is associated with the air element and symbolized by the swift, shimmering presence of the hummingbird. Just picture one: a powerful energetic being, seemingly liberated from the weight of the material world, free of gravity. In Andean cosmology, hummingbirds are honored as messengers between worlds, bridging the spiritual and material planes. The Quechua word for this living energy is *wayra*. The hummingbird is symbolic of this energy. Wayra is the subtle but powerful energy that bridges the material and spiritual dimensions of existence. We experience it in our very breath, with each inhale and exhale even if we are not aware of it; in the wind that rustles the trees, in the ocean waves crashing upon the shore. It is the animated presence of existence, alive within us as our vital life-force energy.

When we call in the North, we are invoking spiritual clarity and asking for direction on our path. A key aspect of integration is bringing spiritual insight down-to-earth making the visions, understandings, and transmissions received in ceremony real and embodied in our lives.

One of the great tasks in this aspect of integration is learning how to dis-identify from the stories and fixed patterns of the thinking mind, so we can listen more clearly to the subtle voice within us. We'll explore this in depth in Chapters 12 though 15.

Anti: East, Fire

Next in the song, I call in Anti, the East direction, which is represented by the fire element and the rising Sun, Taita Inti. The East carries the energies of transformation, willpower, action, and purpose, and is symbolized by the great condor, who soars high above the earth with clarity and power.

The Sun is revered as the source of life, marking the cycles of birth, death, and rebirth. Within the integration process, Taita Inti reminds us that we are always invited into the process of transformation. Fire illuminates, purifies, and brings forth our true essence. In the light of the Sun, we are called to step into authenticity, to let the truth of who we are emerge from the shadows.

Integration is an ongoing initiation into new ways of being. The fire of the east helps us shed what no longer serves, ignite our intentions, and move forward with renewed purpose. In the body, this fire lives at the navel center, which we begin to explore in Chapter 11, as the energetic core of our vitality, courage, and transformation.

Chawpin: The Center

At the center of the chakana, where the four elemental directions converge, lies chawpin—the still point, the space of unity and integration, the sacred center. This center represents the place beyond polarities, beyond duality, where opposites dissolve into harmony.

In many spiritual traditions, this space corresponds to what is called the subtle and/or neutral mind: a spacious inner awareness rooted in presence. Just as the center of the chakana holds and balances all the directions, the neutral mind, especially when empowered by connection to the navel center, allows us to witness our experience without clinging or resisting.

It is here, in the heart of the chakana and the quiet center of our being, that true integration becomes possible, where all parts are welcomed home into wholeness.

The Universal Language of the Elements

Just as the Tibetan mantras and *thangkas* carried the resonance of my first dieta, I also find that the elements of the Andes resonate with the ancient teachings of the East, particularly with yoga and Buddhist teachings. These Andean teachings are not isolated, but universal. Across the sacred traditions of the world, the elements are more than physical forces; they are spiritual archetypes, building blocks of life, and mirrors of consciousness understood as energy.

As we explored earlier, the Four Directions of the chakana represent not only the cardinal points of the physical world but also the elemental energies that shape us internally. The South is the path of earth, connected to the body, Pachamama, and the grounding support of the ancestors. The West flows with the waters of emotion and healing. The East blazes with fire, transformation, and the rising sun. The North carries the winds of air, bringing clarity, communication, and vision. At the center lies chawpin, the sacred still point representing integration and presence.

These elemental archetypes also appear in ancient yoga as the Five Great Elements: *Prithvi* (Earth), *Apas* (Water), *Tejas* (Fire), *Vayu* (Air), and *Akasha* (Ether). In the yogic tradition, these elements exist both in the outer world and within the body-mind. Practices like *asana* (movement), *pranayama* (breathwork), and *dhyana* (meditation) help purify and balance these internal elements, guiding the practitioner toward harmony. Integration, from this view, is not just about processing an experience but about embodying elemental balance as a living expression of wholeness.

Similarly, Tibetan Buddhism offers a refined understanding of the elements as both psychological and spiritual energies. Each element is associated with a specific wisdom and its corresponding emotional shadow. Earth corresponds with equanimity and pride; Water with clarity and attachment; Fire with discernment and aggression; Air with joyful activity and restlessness; and Space with openness and ignorance. Through meditative practice, these energies are transmuted into awakened qualities. The aim, as in other traditions, is to become a conscious participant in the alchemical dance of the elements within.

"We do not 'come into' this world; we come out of it, as leaves from a tree. Every individual is an expression of the whole realm of nature, a unique action of the total universe."

—Alan Watts

Taken together, these traditions affirm a deep and vital truth: the elements are universal teachers. They remind us that nature is not separate from us, it *is* us. Just as trees, rivers, and mountains are composed of earth, water, air, and fire, so too are we. Working with the elements in plant medicine integration is not merely symbolic; it is a direct, embodied pathway back into harmony. Healing becomes not just emotional or physical, but elemental, spiritual, and whole.

Using these elements as a simple, intuitive framework, we can begin to observe what energies within us may be out of balance and gently bring them back into harmony. Some days you may need to lie on the earth and say nothing. Other days you may need to cry, write, dance, or sing. All are valid. The elements are not static: they are fluid, living teachers. Through developing a personal relationship with them, we gain a grounded framework for finding inner balance.

In this elemental map, balance is not a fixed destination but a rhythm, a vibration, much like ceremony itself. Integration is not about improving yourself, but about being in honest relationship with yourself. The more you attune to and harmonize the elemental energies within, the more your life becomes ceremonial. From this place, you don't just carry the medicine, you become it.

In my own life, I consciously attend to these elements each morning through breathwork, yoga, and meditation. Still, there are days when I feel triggered or off center, when my mind is a whirlwind or my heart feels heavy. When that happens, I pause and ask: what element within me needs my attention? If my mind feels chaotic, I breathe into the spacious stillness of the air element and invite calm. If I feel heavy and stuck, I breathe into the water of my heart to invite movement and flow. If I feel anger rising, I acknowledge the fire within and allow it to burn cleanly by naming what's true so that it may release and transform.

Journal Reflection Prompts: Chakana

What does each direction and element tell you about where you are in this moment:

Earth: Are you grounded or scattered?

Water: Are you feeling or avoiding emotion?

Fire: Are you acting or stuck in inertia?

Air: Are you breathing and thinking clearly?

Chawpin/ether: Are you connecting with your inner wisdom, stillness, emptiness?

Self-Exploration Exercise: Integration Ritual - Create a Small Altar

If you don't already have a quiet place to meditate, journal, and reflect with an altar, I suggest creating one in your home. Your altar (or *mesa* as we call it in the lineages that I am a part of) can be a physical reminder and presence in your life, calling you back to the sacred in the busy day-to-day world. As part of your integration journey, you might consider intentionally honoring the four directions by including representations of the elements. I was taught in the Andes to set up my altar with a candle in the East to represent fire, a rock or crystal in the South for earth, a seashell in the West for water, and a feather in the North for air. At the center, I place an object that represents my understanding of chawpin—my sacred center—as it intuitively feels for me.

Think of approaching this space in your daily rhythm as you would a sacred ceremony. The invitation is to create your own ceremonial space with unique rituals that support and sustain your journey. However this unfolds for you, let it be personal and meaningful. Light a candle. Burn incense.

Place fresh flowers. Bow in prayer. Keep a regular time each day—perhaps in the early morning or before bed—to connect here.

Creating and bringing ceremony into your daily life through a space like this has a powerful ripple effect. You may begin with a small altar, and soon find yourself making your bed more carefully, watering your plants with a deeper presence, washing your face or combing your hair in a more nurturing way. Every moment holds the possibility of being sacred, a ceremony, a quiet dance with creation. Making life ceremonial takes intention and attention.

The Elements as Teachers: The Wisdom of Dattatreya

In ancient Indian Bhakti and Yoga traditions, there is a touching story of a holy man who walked in deep communion with life itself. His name was Dattatreya, a mystic and sage revered as an embodiment of the divine. When asked who had guided him on his path, Dattatreya replied that he had twenty-four teachers, none of whom were human. His gurus were drawn from the natural world: animals, birds, phenomena, and most significantly, the five great elements: earth, water, fire, air, and ether.

From earth, he learned patience and stability by witnessing the quiet endurance of mountains and the silent generosity of soil. From water, he understood the essence of purity and adaptability, how to nourish without attachment and flow without resistance. Fire taught him transformation and the power to consume and purify, to burn away the false and illuminate truth. Air became a symbol of freedom and detachment, moving through the world untouched, in motion yet grounded in his own rhythm. From ether, Dattatreya realized the mystery of formlessness by becoming aware of the vastness that holds all things without clinging, the openness that allows everything to arise and dissolve.

Dattatreya's wisdom invites us to reimagine the elements not just as forces of nature or energetic principles, but as living guides for integration. In the context of sacred plant medicine and the healing path, the elements offer a map, not to escape the world, but to embody it more deeply. Just as Dattatreya found divinity in the elemental world, we too can learn to listen to earth's grounding pull, water's cleansing tides, fire's alchemical heat, air's clarifying winds, and space's silent witness.

As we move through our integration journey together in this book, we will return to these elements to bring awareness and balance within. We are all comprised of them and when we work toward balance with them as our teachers we then can learn to embody their most desirable manifestation within our beings: earth is grounded and embodied; fire is radiant; water exists in flow with life and represents being open hearted; air is calm and relaxed; ether represents presence.

Bringing these sacred teachings into our lives is not complicated. We want to bring awareness to the state of our inner being and we can start with learning pranayama (breathwork). Here is a simple practice that you can start your day with. I suggest setting a timer for 3 minutes, working up to 11 minutes, and during this time commit to going in. Playing meditative music will support this practice. Your mind might resist and pitch a fit, especially at first, so set the intention to keep coming back to your breath. As this starts to become familiar your mind and emotional bodies will relax. Keep in mind for this to be effective and support you, it takes consistency.

Breathwork/Asana Practice: Long Slow Deep Breathing with Prayer Pose

Sitting in sukhasana, with the hands in the prayer pose mudra at the heart center, invites the elements we are all comprised of to come into balance within us.

Sit in *sukhasana* (cross-legged) or on a firm chair, activate your root bandhah (lock) by pulling up on your pelvic floor and lower belly, (rectum, sex organs, and navel up and in and then gently release but maintain the connection), spine straight, shoulders relaxed, chin slightly tucked. Visualize and embody your spine as one vertical line rising from your pelvic floor all the way up through the crown of your head, so straight that it has no gravitational pull, either forward or back. Place your hands in prayer pose by bringing palms together at your heart center and applying a light pressure. When we practice this prayer pose *mudra*, we are also inviting the elemental energies of earth, water, air, fire, and ether to become more balanced within us.

Start by inhaling deeply through your nose by filling your belly, your sternum, and finally your upper chest, and holding it in. You should be able to feel your belly physically expand. Then exhale completely through your nose, starting with the upper chest, moving back down through the sternum, and finally emptying the belly by drawing it in toward your ribcage. If you do this fully you should feel your diaphragm lift. Hold the breath in on the inhalation and out on the exhalation for as long as you can as you breath in this way. As you practice, create a steady rhythm. As you suspend your breath also suspend your mind by inviting a sense of spaciousness. Practice this breath at least once a day. Working up to eleven minutes is very beneficial. This long slow deep breathing calms your nervous system, balances the sacred elements within you, and grounds you in your body. Pranayama becomes our ally when we practice them such that they become familiar friends and tools. Think of this breathwork as sacred medicine for your life because it is. Approach this practice as an ongoing courtship: a dance with yourself, one that is so simple and accessible.

As we close this chapter, remember we are not separate from the elements, we are made of them. They live in our bones and breath, our emotions and thoughts, our spirit and skin. When we return to these elements as our teachers—by paying attention to how they manifest as energetic forces within—we begin to walk the path of true integration, one that is rooted in nature, alive in experience, and whole in spirit. A ceremony of life.

Chapter Eleven:

Connecting to the Navel Wisdom

"In the vessel of your body, you yourself are the world tree, deep roots in the Earth and a crown of stars. Your essence bridges dimensions."
—Elizabeth S. Eiler

Our next guest that we want to greet and welcome into the integration ceremony of our lives is our body and, more specifically in this chapter, our navel center. As we explored in the last chapter, we are part of Pachamama, comprised of the same elements as all creation. Let's begin with the earth element: our miraculous human bodies. The body is your temple for the ceremony of life, and it is also your gateway to integration. Whatever you are seeking in terms of healing and self-knowledge cannot be attained outside of your body. The inner journey is the journey home to yourself and your body, and its navel center is the critical, often missed entryway to this path.

The Path Begins with the Body

As we explored in the previous chapters, most of us identify the body by its physical form: two hands, two legs, a beating heart, eyes that see, ears that hear. With this surface-level understanding, we often lose connection to the body's more subtle wisdom. We take our bodies for granted and tend to notice them only when something goes wrong like when there is pain, illness, or fatigue. Yet the body is constantly communicating with us in quiet, nuanced ways.

When we attend plant medicine ceremonies, we often begin to experience ourselves differently. The life-force energy within us becomes more tangible. We feel it moving, pulsing, and vibrating, sometimes with awe, sometimes with confusion, often both. This vital energy is connected to our essential self, that part of us that was never born and will never die. If you've ever had an out-of-body experience—during a ceremony or otherwise—you may already have a visceral understanding of what I'm referring to here. Recognizing and cultivating this awareness of life-force energy, and how it is tethered to the body, is a valuable part of integration.

In Western culture, we are heavily conditioned to identify with the mind. Many of us believe that our thoughts define us and that the mind is the seat of the self. But as part of your integration journey, consider this: what if the mind is not who you are? Imagine the mind as the flower of a blooming plant. For that flower to blossom, the roots must be strong and nourished. The life force of the plant doesn't originate in the bloom. It comes from below, from the hidden roots embedded deeply in the soil. That's why we water the roots, not the petals. Likewise, in the journey of integration, we must tend to our roots within the body.

"You simply breathe in and realize you have a body. You smile to your body; You enjoy having a body to sit or walk on the earth and enjoy the earth."

—Thich Nhat Hanh

The second energy center that we often identify with is the heart. This is the place where we connect with our emotions, where we feel love, grief, longing, and joy. Continuing with the plant analogy, the heart center can be seen as the stems and leaves that support the flowering buds. The heart gives structure and nourishment to our emotional expression, just as stems deliver nutrients and hold the flower upright.

But even the strongest stems cannot thrive without healthy roots. For the stems to grow and the flowers to blossom, the plant must be deeply rooted in nourished soil. In the same way, our heart and mind centers can only flourish if our energetic roots are cared for, if our foundational energy, housed in the body, is honored and attended to.

That foundational center is the navel. It is our source of vitality and personal power, yet for many of us, it has been forgotten, ignored, or abandoned. If we want the healing and insights of our plant medicine journeys to truly take root, we must reconnect with this center. Our integration depends on it. Without grounding ourselves in this vital core of life energy, the insights of the heart and the clarity of the mind have no base from which to sustain lasting transformation.

"Our navel holds within us all energy and matter that originated at the beginning of time from a single point, inflated into the known universe."

—Osho

After exploring the elemental map of the self where we looked at earth's grounding energy, water's fluid energy, air's clearing energy, fire's transformative energy, and space's sacred energy of quiet and stillness, we now turn toward the center of transformation. In our human form, this center resides at our navel and is represented by the sun, on which all life depends. In many ancient traditions, this inner fire is representative of the ability to transform and alchemize, and it is the home of willpower, clarity, and action. In yogic teachings, this center holds the power to burn away confusion, awaken confidence, and ignite the energy needed for integration. Here, fire gives us strength, reminding us that transformation requires friction and healing requires courage.

My spiritual name is *Deva Arani,* given to me by a teacher at the very beginning of my spiritual journey. At the time I was a lost and frightened woman, just beginning to understand that to find my way I would have to relinquish everything I thought made me feel safe, loved, and worthy. Yet this teacher saw beyond my fear—beyond the identity I clung to—and named me for the radiant truth of who I could become. *Arani* is a Sanskrit word for the sacred kindling sticks used by ancient wisdom keepers to ignite the divine fire in temple rituals. The story goes that we each carry our own inner *arani*, and through the necessary friction of healing, we can spark our divine flame, illuminating our path and lighting the way for others who seek truth and authenticity. This sacred spark lives within our navel center, the core of our courage and will. It is from this place that we learn to burn away illusion and remember who we truly are.

Friction Occurs at the Navel Center

Each of us as humans are graced with a life energy that is tethered to our bodies through our navel centers. The navel center resides in our physical bodies, and through our physical bodies we can strengthen and connect to that life-giving energy.

"Cultivate the root, the leaves and branches will take care of themselves."

—Confucius

The navel is our first center, the original point of connection, nourishment, and life. In the womb, it is through the umbilical cord that we are physically connected to our mother and receive her sustenance. Indeed, before our heart beats or the brain begins to form, the navel sustains us. It is the primal thread through which we are woven into life. In many ancient teachings, it is also said that when the soul leaves the body, it exits through the navel. The navel is both our first and final portal.

To begin our integration journey at the navel center is to return to our original source of life. It is a way of rooting the vastness of our experience into the body—into a place that existed within us before our outer identities—our minds took charge of our beings. The navel is the anchor in our integration journey.

The navel center is woven throughout the teachings of ancient yogis, saints, sages, and wisdom keepers. Patanjali, known as the father of yoga, was an ancient Indian sage who lived around the 2nd century BC. He wrote the *Yoga Sutras,* which are the foundation of all the various yoga forms we know and practice today. In Patanjali's Yoga Sutras, it is said that through meditation on the navel one gains deep knowledge of the body's constitution. This speaks to the navel as a gateway to embodied wisdom, which is required for our integration to take root in our beings.

Later yogic traditions expanded on Patanjali's teachings. The *manipura* chakra at the navel governs digestion, transformation, and will. The Hatha Yoga *Pradipika*[11] describes it this way: "When the fire burns in the region of the navel, the nectar from the moon in the head flows downward and is consumed. Thus, the yogi is freed from disease, and his body becomes firm." This teaching describes the fire of *agni,* not only to metabolize food, but to digest experience, emotion, and ego. A balanced navel center gives rise to self-trust, emotional resilience, and inner strength.

In Kundalini Yoga, the third chakra, also known as the *nabhi* or navel point, is considered the powerhouse of prana, our vital life force. It is here that the dormant kundalini energy is nourished and stabilized before it can safely rise. Through focused breathwork, core activation, and meditative awareness at the navel, we ignite our inner fire, cultivating clarity, willpower, and spiritual stamina. Without a strong navel center, our kundalini energy cannot rise in balance. In this tradition, the navel is the command center: the radiant core of action, direction, and destiny.

In ancient Taoist philosophy, the energy center just below the navel is called the lower *dantian* or the cauldron of life force (*qi*). It is cultivated through breath and stillness and serves as the energetic root of the Tao within us. Here, to return to the dantian is to harmonize with the flow of life itself, where action arises from stillness and strength is found in yielding.

"The heavy is the root of the light. The still is the master of the restless. Therefore the wise stay rooted in the belly of stillness."

—Lao Tzu

Osho, contemporary mystic, spoke often of the navel as the original center of being. He taught that living from the navel was a way to live in

11 Svatmarama. Hatha Yoga Pradipika. Translated by Brian Dana Akers. Woodstock, NY: YogaVidya.com, 2002.

presence, that connection to the navel allows us to respond to life directly rather than react from the mind.

"The navel is your original center. The head is a created center. If you want to find the truth, go to the navel."

—Osho

Not surprisingly, the Andean wisdom keepers also emphasize the navel center. The name Cusco, means *navel of the world*. This reflects the understanding that just as Cusco was the center of the Inca empire, our navel is the center of our human form. Within the human body, the navel is where we engage in *ayni*, sacred reciprocity with Pachamama and the cosmos, which is the central core relationship that all beings should aspire to develop within themselves.

"From the center, life expands. From the center, we enter relationship with the worlds above and below. The navel is where we weave the threads between the seen and unseen."

—Q'ero elder

To begin the path of integration at the navel is to root the medicine of our journey in the place where we were first nourished, where our lives began. It is to remember the first rhythm we ever knew before thought, before language, before we became "I." By returning to this sacred center, we gather ourselves to commence our integration journey with a firm foundation to support and sustain our intentions; and longing to heal and understand who we are in the mystery that is life.

The navel center is located a few inches below the belly button. It is an energetic lighthouse within the body. Ancient yogis taught that 72 energy meridians emanate from the navel, spanning into 72,000 energy channels throughout the body. This is where *prana* (life force) and *apana* (eliminating force) are balanced.

In Western culture, we've forgotten this. The language and understanding of the navel as a vital energy center and source of inner intelligence has been lost. We intuit its importance when we say things like "trust your gut" or "my gut response is..." but otherwise, we overlook this ancient wisdom. Our children are taught to develop their minds. We learn about our hearts through relationships and emotional growth, but the language of the navel has fallen silent. This is why we begin here—because when we reconnect with the navel center, our integration work can truly land and take root.

We must move our attention downward from the mind and heart, to the navel: our source of life energy. We must tend to and connect with our roots. When life force energy stagnates below the navel, our minds and emotions become reactive, anxious, depressed, and overstimulated by the external world. When we bring awareness to the navel, we return to presence. This connection becomes an anchor and entryway to the internal space of awareness. It is the doorway to meditation, and meditation is the doorway to integration.

Integration requires that we relax the mind and tend to the heart. But we cannot tell the mind to be still. We cannot force emotional regulation through knowledge alone. We need a back door, and in the human form, that door is the navel center.

Physiologically, breath is the most powerful way to connect with the navel. The deeper we breathe, the more we awaken and nourish this center. As we explored in the last chapter, deep rhythmic breathing while sitting, walking, or working can shift your state entirely. Your breath follows your thoughts and emotions, but your thoughts and emotions will also follow your breath. When you consciously breathe deeply, your mind begins to quiet, your emotions soften, and the breath can travel deeper still, reaching the navel and watering it with the nourishment it needs.

This takes attention, intention, and persistence. But if you stay with it, this deep, even breath will become your natural rhythm. From that rhythm, your life energy will begin to radiate from your navel. When the energy of your navel center is awakened, you will begin to feel energy flowing throughout your entire being.

In Chapter Ten, we explored the long, slow, deep breath as a gateway to awareness. Now, we deepen that practice with another pranayama.

Breathwork/Asana Practice: Breath of Fire

Gyan mudra, also known as the wisdom seal, enhances wisdom, mental clarity, and focus. It involves touching the tip of the index finger to the tip of the thumb while keeping the other three fingers extended. This mudra stimulates the brain, improves concentration, and promotes a sense of calm and openness.

Sit in sukhasana or on a firm chair. Activate your root lock by pulling up on your pelvic floor and lower belly, (rectum, sex organs and navel up and in and then gently release but maintain the connection) keep your spine straight, shoulders relaxed, and chin slightly tucked. Visualize and embody your spine as one vertical line rising from your pelvic floor all the way up through the crown of your head, so straight that it has no gravitational pull, either forward or back. Place your hands in Gyan mudra with thumb and index finger connected in the wisdom seal and other fingers extended straight and place them on your knees, with arms extended, but relaxed.

If you want a more challenging experience hold your arms up at a sixty-degree angle with thumbs extended and fingers folded and practice for three minutes. This might seem hard at first but if you can push through the threshold that this creates within your body your energy also will move, flow and release. It is a necessary and healing friction.

From either of these two positions, we begin the breath of fire.

By holding our arms up at a 60-degree angle with our thumbs extended while doing breath of fire, we create pressure that might feel uncomfortable if we stay with it for the full three minutes. However, when we push through this discomfort, we also push through an energy threshold that than allows energy that is stuck below the navel center to become unblocked and move upward.

To learn breath of fire, begin by sticking your tongue out and panting like a dog. Pant with a steady rhythm and notice if you can feel your navel center engaging. The panting should be light enough that it's sustainable, yet firm enough to feel a gentle internal pressure. Once you've found a consistent rhythm and can sense the navel pumping, bring your tongue back in and continue the breath through your nose. Each inhale and exhale should be equal in force and pace. Your navel is the pump, actively involved in each breath.

You can use this technique any time during the day, especially if you feel scattered or stuck. Whether panting through your mouth or nose, this rhythmic breathing invites movement into your energetic system. Breath of fire has many benefits: it stirs stuck energy, increases vitality, and helps sharpen mental focus. But here, we are most interested in its ability to gently but effectively activate the navel center. Let your awareness anchor itself in the breath and its rhythm. If your mind begins to wander, return to the breath and the pumping of the navel focusing on the cadence of movement. Music, especially rhythmic drumming, can support this practice.

Pranayama becomes a true ally when practiced regularly. Over time, these breath techniques become familiar friends and accessible tools for daily life. If we want to access our internal and continuous connection to life force energy, we must awaken and recharge our navel energy center. Breath of fire is a simple, effective way to support this intention.

The Navel Center Is the Home of Courage

"Nature loves courage. You make the commitment and nature will respond to that commitment by removing impossible obstacles. Dream the impossible dream and the world will not grind you under, it will lift you up. This is the trick. This is what all these teachers and philosophers who really counted, who really touched the alchemical gold, this is what they understood. This is the shamanic dance in the waterfall. This is how magic is done. By hurling yourself into the abyss and discovering it's a feather bed."

—Terence McKenna

Integration requires courage. Courage resides in the navel center. This energy is circular because when you practice courage, you strengthen your navel center. When you strengthen your navel center, your courage deepens. We experience fear in the body first, and often it registers at the navel center. For example, recently I was startled by a large moose standing just outside the front door of my mountain cabin. The first sensation I felt was my stomach dropping. Before my mind could catch up, my body had already registered the fear. This is how fear dwells in the body: hidden like roots beneath the soil of our awareness in our navel. Since fear lives in the navel center, it makes sense that our true courage arises from this same place.

Most of us have adapted to fear from an early age by denying it, pushing it down, or pretending it isn't there. When left unacknowledged, fear lingers beneath the surface, shaping unconscious patterns of avoidance and projection. Physically, this repression often shows up as shallow breathing and voices that lack depth or resonance. We disconnect from our center, from our strength. To access and develop our true courage, we must reconnect with the navel center.

This begins with deep breathing, as we've been exploring. Another practice is to bring awareness to our voices. Speak from your navel center. You've likely been around people whose voices are high, rapid, or breathy—energetically scattered, insecure, or fearful. When you ground your voice in your navel center, it carries the energy of strength and presence. Play with this. Be curious. Notice where your voice originates and how it feels to speak from your navel. This is a subtle but powerful shift, one that doesn't require a jungle retreat or mountaintop monastery, just presence in your daily life.

To live your life as ceremony requires courage, as does integration. The disintegrated parts of us—those we've exiled or abandoned—need healing and reintegration. These parts were exiled for a reason. As young children, we encountered moments too painful or overwhelming to fully process, so we split off from the authentic moment to protect ourselves. Now, to bring those pieces back into wholeness takes tremendous courage. That courage grows from within the navel center.

Journal Reflection Prompts: Courage

What does fear feel like in your body?

What does courage feel like in your body?

Explore by remembering a time you were afraid, and you pushed through the fear.

Explore by remembering a time you were afraid, and you did not push through the fear.

What fears do you currently wrestle with in your life?

Bring awareness to the fears or doubts held in your navel.

Ask yourself, what are you afraid of that you can move through today?

"As I said, if a situation of fear arises then it is felt first at the navel center. So, the more one practices fearlessness, the healthier one's navel will become; and the more one practices courage, the more one's navel center will develop. The more fearlessness grows, the stronger and healthier the navel will be – and the deeper ones contact with life. That is why all the great meditators of the world have considered fearlessness to be an essential quality in a seeker; fearlessness has no other significance. The significance of fearlessness is that it makes the navel center totally alive; it is instrumental in the total development of the navel."

—Osho

Discipline and Commitment Reside at the Navel Center

Not only will you strengthen your courage by connecting with the navel center, but this is also where you can cultivate discipline and commitment. These qualities are essential for creating real growth and expansion in your life. The navel center holds the strength required to change, to move through resistance, and to fuel perseverance. Perseverance matters because as we've explored, resistance is often propelled by the familiar currents of old patterns and habits. Every step you take toward integration carries the energy of the new, and that energy is often met with an equal and opposite pull toward the old. This is the moment of choice.

The ability to choose a new path rather than stay on the familiar, lackluster one is rooted in the navel center. It takes discipline to nourish yourself, to tend to self-care, and to return to presence again and again. And yet, as you connect more deeply with this center, you may find that the negative patterns and behaviors you once struggled against begin to lose their grip without force. The positive changes you long to embody begin to take shape naturally, not through striving, but through alignment. This is the quiet strength of the navel center: it empowers transformation from within.

"Be strong then, and enter into your own body; there you have a solid place for your feet."

—Kabir

Strong Center, Lifted Heart

When I was in my early thirties, I was training for my first marathon and worked with a dear English triathlete named Mark, who was in Boulder training for the Olympics. He was charming, funny, and incredibly inspiring, and I'll admit, I had quite the crush on him. One of the first things Mark taught me was proper running form: heart lifted, shoulders down, chin slightly tucked—exactly like in sukhasana pose. He explained that if I ran with hunched shoulders and my head jutting forward, as so many people do, I wouldn't be able to access my full lung capacity. His signature reminder was to shout, "Run proud!" whenever my posture started to collapse.

Looking back, I realize that to run with a lifted heart, I had to engage my navel center. It was the strength of my core that supported my spine, allowing my heart to open and lift. Integration may be a very different kind of marathon, but the lesson still applies. "Run proud" is another way of saying: connect to your center, move from your navel, let your heart rise supported by your inner strength.

Breathwork/Asana Practice: Mountain Pose, Standing and Walking

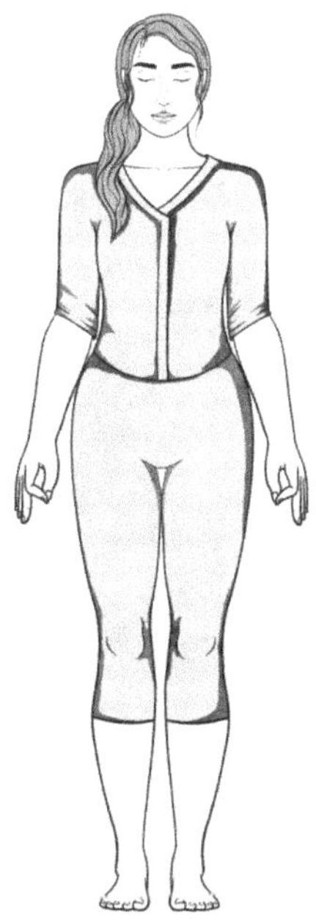

We can connect to our navel by practicing tadasana, or mountain pose, throughout our day. Standing with connection to our navel, our hearts lifted, our shoulders down, will not only improve our overall sense of well-being but also connect us to our navel wisdom.

In practical terms, physical asanas require bringing awareness to your posture. First, learn *tadasana*. Standing with feet hip width apart, lift and spread your toes, connecting them to the Earth. Remember sukhasana? The same principles of alignment with gravity are practiced here. We start by pulling up on our root lock, gently pulling in our navel, chest lifted, shoulders down, and chin slightly tucked. Imagine one vertical line that is connected to the earth through your feet and the sky through your crown chakra. Let your arms hang loosely at your sides, fingers relaxed. Come back to this posture, practice as you move through your everyday life. Stand regally, as if you're in ceremony.

Next practice walking from this asana. Allow your arms to swing gently at your sides and try placing your hands in gyan mudra with your thumb gently connected to your index finger on each hand. Make this a walking meditation. Bring attention to the navel point and notice that it is the access point from which the movement flows and the vertical line is held as you walk. Gently, steadily. The form initiated from the navel center creates stability in your body, and this stability then influences your other centers. Ideally, walk for 20 minutes or more every day in this posture, leading from the navel. Practice it as you move through your day whenever you remember.

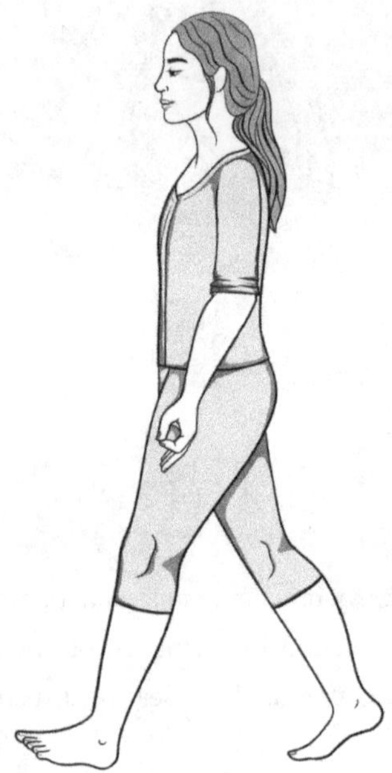

Placing our hands in gyan mudra while walking is a practice that reminds us to move from the navel and be in presence.

Our navel center is also strengthened through proper diet, restorative sleep, and physical work. What this looks like will differ for each of us, but as part of your integration journey, consider the energetic quality of what you consume. Notice what foods feel nourishing and supportive, what feels comforting but perhaps dulling, and what feels heavy or depleting, including alcohol and other substances. For me, the less processed my food, the more natural and whole my nourishment, the more I feel attuned to the true bounty of Pachamama. I used to carry protein bars with me on hikes, but over the years I've replaced them with whole foods like nuts and fresh fruit like apples, bananas, and oranges that are just as portable, have no packaging, and feel more healing to me because of their direct connection to nature.

Sleep is a vital, stabilizing force for the entire system. Make it a priority. I know many people struggle with sleep, and if that's true for you, I gently encourage you to seek support—whatever that looks like—because sleep is essential for grounding, emotional balance, and nervous system restoration.

By physical work, I mean anchoring ourselves in simple, ordinary tasks: washing dishes, sweeping the floor, folding laundry, tending the yard. These daily acts are opportunities to engage your breath, presence, and effort. Grit is cultivated through effort, and when we bring conscious engagement to these small physical tasks, we move energy through the body. This strengthens the navel center.

Practice keeping a gentle awareness of your navel throughout the day. At first, it takes effort and intention, but over time it becomes more natural. With this connection, you'll likely find that more life energy is available to you. Remind yourself: I can work with my life energy, tend to my vitality, and build momentum through this connection to my core.

When we lose connection to our navel center, we lose access to the life energy that surrounds and supports us. The sun, the moon, the stars, the breath of the Earth—these are living presences offering energy and guidance. But we can only receive them if we are receptive. When we are not connected to our navel center, we are like a flower trying to grow in the shade. We can't fully bloom for lack of direct sunlight. When we reawaken the fire at the navel, we open to the sun within, reconnecting with purpose, vitality, and the sacred rhythm of nature. This is the radiant thread that runs through the ceremony of integration: not just remembering who we are but embodying it fully through connection to ourselves and the natural rhythm of existence.

"The navel is the center and not the heart or the brain.... Keep searching within and bring your consciousness to the level of the navel center. That is the first step of sadhana. When you walk, keep your attention on the navel. When you sit, keep your mind on the navel; when you get up, be aware of the navel. Do what you will, but let your consciousness always move around the navel."

—Lao Tzu

Chapter Twelve:

The Multifaceted Nature of Mind and Integration

"The most difficult thing for spiritual seekers to do is to stop struggling, striving, seeking, and searching. Why? Because in the absence of struggle you don't know who you are; you lose your boundaries, you lose your separateness, you lose your specialness, you lose the dream you have lived all your life. Eventually, you lose everything that your mind has created and awaken to who you truly are: the fullness of freedom, unbound by any identifications, identities, or boundaries."

—Adyashanti

Now that we have some sense of the navel center and its power to ground and stabilize our integration journey, let's turn to the role our mind plays in this process. Here, we are invited to meet the mind with curiosity and respect, as a guest in the ceremony of our lives. The mind is multifaceted, multilayered, and shaped by the elements of air, fire, and water in both yogic and Indigenous traditions. It is a guest that needs attention, compassion, and understanding. Most importantly, we must signal to it that it is not in charge of our life ceremony, but instead plays a supporting role, in balance with our whole being.

During the integration process the mind can be tricky terrain. One of the most profound revelations in plant medicine work is the realization that we are not who we thought we were. The spiritual journey asks us to recognize that we are not our minds. This truth is ancient and deep; it may take many lifetimes to fully embody. In ceremony, we may have touched this directly and viscerally with a sense of mysterious familiarity. But when we return to our ordinary state of consciousness, the mind often scrambles to reassert its authority. One of the biggest struggles and deepest fears that arise during the ceremony is the surrender of control. Letting go of the mind and releasing our grip on control can be terrifying. Yet it is also the portal to healing. Our relationship with this surrender—our capacity to release the mind's dominance—is a central thread in our integration process.

As we return from ceremony, the mind often rushes to make sense of the experience, trying to create a cohesive narrative. This is not inherently wrong; it's a form of self-protection. But if left unchecked, the mind's effort to regain control can suppress the truth we touched in ceremony: that we are so much more than our minds. One of the central tasks of integration is to bring this deeper knowing back online after our ceremony experience has concluded.

Ah, the mind. For integration to truly take root, we must develop a capacity to be with uncertainty, to rest in not knowing. And the mind does not like this. Dis-identification from the mind is both the path of meditation and the essence of integration. The mind creates an inner tension, one that inevitably surfaces during the integration process. The mind is challenged to make sense of a non-ordinary experience within the confines of ordinary reality. It is tasked with integrating a spiritual, multidimensional encounter into a three-dimensional world. How do you integrate an experience of being out of time or out of body if the mind has no blueprint for it? And yet, when integration is successful, that very experience transforms our perception and expands our understanding of reality.

The mind dislikes the unfamiliar. It seeks to categorize, define, and interpret. Its goal is to make the unknown known, to feel safe. But integration asks us to remain open to mystery. It challenges the mind to make space for the unknowable. This requires us to take a step back from our thoughts, to observe the mind without fully identifying with it.

Practically speaking, the mind plays an important role. Its task is to help us derive meaning from our experience, to create a coherent narrative that supports growth and healing. When the experience fits within a current narrative, this process can feel seamless. But when our experience introduces repressed memories, unfamiliar symbols, or contradicts our beliefs, integration becomes more challenging. Still, the mind is a valuable tool. The danger lies not in using the mind, but in letting it take over. When the mind becomes the sole interpreter of our experience, we limit ourselves. We cut ourselves off from the deeper, embodied, nonlinear layers of truth that can only be accessed through presence.

The mind is the depository of our lived experience. It helps us function in the world. But it is not the master of our being, it is a servant. In integration, we are learning to embody this wisdom.

Let's explore this here. First, understand that we are often on autopilot. Our minds function for the most part automatically. This automation is comprised of endless thoughts: focused or flowing, repetitive or obsessive, bouncing around the past or present, sometimes dark, sometimes humorous; but always in flux. Our thoughts live in our minds like a hive of honeybees: sometimes busy, sometimes playful, sometimes supportive, and sometimes distressed or disturbed. Thoughts come and go, buzzing and landing.

For instance, as we think about our ceremony, we might have thoughts like: *Was that real? Why did that person say that to me afterward? I hope I wasn't too loud. I don't think I did that right. What did that mean? Who am I?* And on and on. We can stay in this loop of rumination if we choose, but it's not helpful. This is living in our minds on autopilot.

Another primary function of the mind is as a protective shield. It creates a perceived reality that allows us to remain entangled with the outside world and avoid our inner one. In essence, we escape our internal world by living in our heads.

When the mind is in charge, we form an identity based on how we want others to see us. We present ourselves as this person so consistently that we start to believe that this outer image, crafted by the mind, is who we truly are. We live accordingly. We become entangled outside of ourselves: seeking approval, acceptance, and love through the false narrative created by the mind.

We don't realize these are masks or identities we developed to be safe—to be loved and to fit in. They were shaped in our early years to survive and prevent abandonment. All our energy is projected outward to maintain these masks, avoiding the pain inside us that actually needs attention and compassion. We escape the real fears of abandonment, unworthiness, disconnection, and loneliness by projecting a persona that seems to have none of these wounds. In doing so, we disconnect from our true selves.

This outer projection becomes so habitual, so ingrained, that it seems real. One of the greatest fears of inner work is discovering that the outer charade is not real; it's a performance, a lie we inherited and adopted. To turn inward requires us to see ourselves without the masks: the fear, the jealousy, the anger, the resentment, all the feelings deemed unacceptable are hidden within.

It takes tremendous courage to turn inward and see.

In my own life, I've met with this resistance and discomfort. In my early thirties, I started long-distance running. This was my first entry into meditation. My outer intention was to prove my worth by becoming a marathoner, tracking my mileage and times with pride. But on those long runs, something shifted. A new rhythm emerged, a relaxed, steady cadence between breath, body, and mind. I began to recognize this not just as a runner's high but as a deeper inner potential, and when I wasn't in this peaceful state, I longed for it.

I began a meditation practice, and though it was difficult, I persisted mainly because, underneath it all, I was miserable. On the outside, my life looked normal, happy, successful. But I came to realize it wasn't *my* life. The person I showed to the world was a mask. Beneath that mask lived a frightened, traumatized, angry being, and the more I tried to ignore her, the louder she became.

Eventually, I broke. I began working with a wise elder therapist. In our first session, I cried real tears that burst from the dam I had built inside me. The first words out of my mouth were: "My whole life is one big fat lie!" And at that time, it felt true. My desire to be loved, to feel safe and to belong, had forced me to construct a persona that was coming apart at the seams. I was terrified. And yet, I had to begin there, with that raw truth, so I could start learning who I was without the masks that had helped me survive.

We must see ourselves with courage and without judgment. We censor ourselves, and the parts we hide from view are pushed beneath the surface. The mind labels these parts as bad or fixed, so we suppress them. We must teach our minds to meet these parts with curiosity, compassion, and the understanding that they are fluid.

Integration is when our inner being matches our outer expression. We drop the presentation; we drop the scripts. That's authenticity, and that's integration.

Understanding who we are *not* is one of the greatest catalysts for transformation. That's why the sacred medicine journey is so powerful—it offers a glimpse of who we really are beneath the layers. It puts us in direct contact with our true self, beyond the mask. It reconnects us to something infinite, and we long to stay in that place of unmasked connection. That connection is what we lose when we adopt false identities.

There are many ways to understand the mind, across philosophies, schools of psychology, and spiritual traditions. But the first and most important truth is this: *You are not your mind*.

Meditation is the practice of separating from the mind, disidentifying with it, so we can access the subtler energies of our true self, our inner wisdom, intuition, and presence. You must decide who you want in charge of your integration. To make that choice consciously, it helps to understand the nature of your mind.

In the next chapters, we'll explore the mind from several perspectives. Think of it as untangling a large knot: by teasing out one thread at a time, we can gain insight without becoming overwhelmed by the whole.

Preferences

First, let's talk about preferences. The mind is like a hive of worker bees! One of the mind's primary jobs is to define and make sense of our worlds, and it does this largely through comparing and contrasting. The mind has preferences based on our experiences in life, like our conditionings. Something is good, something is bad. I like this and I don't like that. Becoming aware of our preferences is an excellent tool for starting to see our minds. Try it. As you move through your day start to pay attention to your preferences without judgment, but instead with curiosity. Pay particular attention to preferences about yourself. Who you should be, how you should act, what you should do, what you should look like. As you realize that your mind is constantly comparing, contrasting, liking, and disliking, remember to breathe into your navel and see if you can shift your narrative into a more neutral mode.

When I visit the jungle for dieta, there's a specific tambo that I stay in. One year due to timing I went with a new group of friends, and arrived to discover that all of the tambos had already been pre-selected and my tambo was not available. Mature medicine woman that I was, I found myself seething and felt waves of frustration and anger, at the perceived unfairness of it all. My preference created an expectation within me, and this disappointed expectation was a trigger that fed my mind. There I was at the start of my pilgrimage in the jungle, my most sacred home, miserable. As with the medicine's intrinsic wisdom, shortly into the first ceremony this preference disappeared as I realized that the tambo I was in had been specifically designated for me and my needs for this diet. My mind relaxed, the emotions softened, my heart opened. Whew. I share this story as an example of the relationship between mind and preference, and how preferences surface from our past rather than present.

If we can look within and not ascribe preferences about our outer world and the state of our beings, we are training our minds to relax. Having preferences creates tension between what is and what we think should be. Our minds are actively scripting our lives to keep us safe in our outer worlds, accepted, included, liked, loved, and our mind directs that we act a certain way to ensure this flow. But as these scripts are extrinsically motivated, they incite a *false* energy flow, one that likely began in infancy when we learned certain behaviors garnered favorable responses from our caregivers. We want to change that script to allow authenticity. Paying attention to our preferences allows us to see the script and let it go.

I remember hearing Pema Chodron give a talk years ago where she described visiting a friend in the hospital who had lost a leg. She asked the friend how she was, and the friend said, "I'm terrible, can't you see I just had my leg amputated?" Pema replied, "Ah, you lost your leg. What is the problem?" I think of this whenever my need to prefer really kicks in, as a gentle reminder.

Our Beliefs

"My technique is don't believe anything. If you believe in something, you are automatically precluded from believing its opposite."
—Terence McKenna

We are filled with beliefs: religious beliefs, political beliefs, ancestral beliefs about how to live, what is good, and what is bad. Beliefs are imposed upon us from outside of ourselves. Once we believe something, the mind holds it as a fixed truth. That belief becomes rigid and tense. Our experiences are then shaped and limited by these beliefs, pulling us away from fluidity, flexibility, and responsiveness.

If I believe something to be true without having directly experienced it myself, then it's a mind mechanism. This mechanism feeds other mechanisms such as comparison, competition, separation, and superiority. This nourishes the ego-mind with even more beliefs, like believing people who don't share our beliefs are wrong, inferior, or dangerous. This is how the mind creates chaos, both within us and in the world around us.

Be wary of beliefs that are not rooted in your direct experience.

Your own experience is felt as a truth throughout your being. It doesn't require effort to maintain. It doesn't need defending. We don't need to convert others or convince anyone. We simply know. Wisdom comes through personal experience—not through belief or knowledge passed down by others.

In terms of integration, remember that your medicine experience is beyond your belief system, beyond belief altogether. It's important not to try to wrap a belief system around the experience afterward. Our beliefs, no matter how fixed or deeply ingrained, live in the periphery of the mind. Integration invites us deeper into presence, not ideology.

The Peripheral Mind

When I work with my clients in integration sessions, I often help them distinguish between the center and the periphery of the mind. I use the analogy of the sun and its rays. In this analogy, the sun itself represents the neutral, subtle mind, while the periphery is made up of all the aspects that manifest through our preferences, beliefs, adaptive patterns, ego identifications, and projections. The periphery is in essence who we *think* we are—our ego identities—shaped by conditioning and story. Part of the integration process is recognizing that these identities are not who we truly are.

I've been blessed to participate in Zen *satori* meditation on different non-medicine retreats over the years, and for me it has been a powerful way to understand and experience this distinction. In satori, we are given a koan—an unanswerable question—such as, "Tell me who you are?" and we repeat it again and again for hours, days, even weeks. *Who am I?* "I am a woman living on planet Earth. I am an attorney. I am a gardener. I am human...." As we answer, friction arises because we are naming the periphery, layer by layer, until it is stripped away. At some point, there's a shift. We begin to realize what we are *not*. *Neti neti:* Not this, not that. What remains is silence, presence. Here resides the subtle mind.

"In the search of who you are not the reality of who you are emerges by itself."

—Sri Nisargadatta Maharaj

Another way of understanding the subtle mind is to consider that there are two types of thinking. One arises from our periphery. When we think from the periphery, we are caught in a powerful energy vortex shaped by our past and future. The energy from these thoughts becomes stuck within our bodies as patterned tension. Periphery thinking halts energy flow. Our chattering minds create pressure in our beings because the thoughts here are repetitive, circulating in loops. Becoming aware of our periphery is essential, for this is where our minds run amok. This is where our lives can spin out of alignment. And it's also where our integration can derail. Our periphery hijacks our awareness, pulling us into stories, narratives, beliefs, and projections.

When we bring awareness to this, we can begin to dis-identify and access another way of thinking, through the subtle mind. This more subtle way of thinking is a positive energetic current that flows and does not get stuck. The subtle mind is the awareness we want guiding our integration process.

When we dis-identify from the periphery, we create space for the subtle mind to help steer our lives. A kind of inner relaxation occurs, allowing us to witness and heal the unconscious experiences from our early years that fuel the periphery's patterns.

The periphery mind holds all the adaptive beliefs and behaviors we took on to survive, to be loved, and to feel safe. This is where our inner child resides, often still fighting to protect us. We want to bring gentle awareness and compassion to the periphery so that the subtle mind can gain traction and become accessible. The peripheral mind is actually quite fragile. Like rays from the sun, it has no form and yet we think it is who we are and let it steer our lives.

Picture the sun as you might have drawn it as a child: a circle with lines radiating out from it. That circle is your presence, your awareness, your being here now. This is your subtle mind. Imagine you are on a walk, and you see a blooming lilac. You take in its color, its scent, the dew on its petals and you feel awe, wonder, joy. In that moment of presence, you are in the center, the sun itself. That is ceremony.

Now, notice what happens when the periphery takes over: I love lilacs. This is my favorite color. I remember the lilac bush where the butterflies swarmed. That's where we buried Kali. The butterflies are an endangered species. The planet is dying. My grandmother loved lilacs. I disappointed her. I'm unlovable, and on it goes.

If you can catch this cascade, witness it with compassion and return to the moment—the scent of lilac, the color, the air on your skin—you return to the center. You return to presence. And in that moment, you are integrated.

Simple. Not easy.

To get a more substantial feel for what I mean by the periphery, it's helpful to look at our identities. How do you label yourself? For example: strong, weak, a leader, a follower, an introvert, an extrovert, outgoing, shy, sensitive, crazy, solid, free-spirited, an old soul, a young soul? How might others label you? Generous, frugal, kind, unfriendly, shallow, deep, dim, smart, reliable, undependable?

Another key to understanding the labels of the peripheral mind is recognizing that certain archetypal energies live here as well. These archetypes can unconsciously shape our behavior and perception. For instance, we might carry a strong victim archetype. In this case, our mind's response to challenges is, "It's not my fault," or "I'm not responsible," or "Why is this happening to me?" If the martyr archetype is dominant, we might feel, "I have to do everything myself," or "No one else can be relied upon." The prostitute archetype can show up when we sell ourselves short to be loved or accepted—saying yes when we want to say no or compromising our truth for belonging. The beggar archetype might manifest as a sense of scarcity or emptiness, constantly seeking to be filled through others, often without reciprocity.

Our inner critic is another powerful force in the periphery. It often works hand in hand with these archetypes, amplifying their voices and judgments. It deserves to be seen and met, like all the others, with awareness and compassion. Its energy is fierce and worthy of our attention on this path.

Self-Exploration Exercise: Tell Me Who You Are Zen Koan Exercise

This is an exercise to help to recognize the peripheral mind and bring awareness to the patterns that it creates in our lives, so they may be witnessed, challenged, and reframed in alignment with integration. To do this exercise you will need a quiet, comfortable space, a mirror, your journal, 30 minutes, and an open, curious mindset.

1. Set a timer for ten minutes. Spend this time gazing at yourself in the mirror and asking yourself "Tell me who you are?" Then answer out loud. Each time your answer seems complete, repeat the question. Maintain eye contact with yourself in the mirror. Be totally honest and present in each response. Continue until your timer goes off.

2. Now, if it feels right, make a list of all the ideas that your mind has about who you are. Include in this list the above archetypes, even if you're not sure you identify with them, and your inner child, even if this idea seems unfamiliar or silly to you. These archetypes are universal, and it is so good to bring awareness to them with curiosity. Once you have compiled this list, read through it and ask yourself, "Is this who I am?"

3. Next, identify where these parts of yourself come from in your history. I realized I was shy in kindergarten, a leader in high school, etc. For the archetypes, see if you can identify when they started operating in your being. Don't judge any of this: instead, be playful and bring in humor and compassion.

4. Now, next to each descriptor add an opposite word; for instance, if you listed shy, write outgoing next to it.

5. Ask yourself, where can your life force energy easily flow and where is it stuck amongst these identities. Not sure? Take some time and look in. It might be easy to identify as shy, but can you also see that at times you are quite outgoing? It might be easy to identify as a follower, but can you see where in your life you lead or long to lead? Keep going.

Our personalities are not fixed, and we encompass all the polarities within. Our journey is to recognize this so that our minds can relax and not tighten around the false notions about who we think we are. This helps us to understand that our personality is not who we are. This is another way of understanding our mind and dis-identifying from it.

Your Inner Child Resides in Your Periphery

We all have an inner child that longs for attention and attunement. This inner child learned to act a certain way to please and fit into the family and societal structures he/she was born into. Our inner child's natural inclinations to flow and trust was stymied and corrected in well-meaning ways by our parents, teachers, and other elders to keep us safe. Those of us who experienced trauma in our childhoods have an extra hurt inner child needing attention and comfort. When we attune to our inner child's unmet needs, we find healing and connection. This is important for integration.

Self-Exploration Exercise: Meeting Our Inner Child

One gentle, yet profound, method for accessing the voices of our inner child is writing with the nondominant hand. This practice invites a direct conversation between the logical, organizing adult self (usually associated with the dominant hand), and the tender, intuitive, feeling self (which can express through the non-dominant hand and yes, I can attest it does want to be heard). When we slow down and write with the hand we don't normally use, we open a channel to our inner child who hides within and "anonymously" fuels our periphery mind.

Because it requires us to use the hand that is not associated with writing, non-dominant handwriting can feel surprisingly awkward at first and that's part of its power. The unfamiliar movement mirrors the vulnerability of our inner child and helps us access states that are less filtered. What emerges may be childlike in tone and I have found that it comes out with messages that are simple, emotional, and direct. This can create a dialogue that honors both the adult self and the tender child, building a bridge between parts of the psyche that have long been disconnected.

In the context of sacred plant medicine integration, this practice offers a way to connect with and understand the needs of your inner child, who also attended ceremony with you. It has been my experience in exploring this myself and also in mentoring others in this work that we can reconnect with early experiences or unmet needs that might have been threads of our ceremony experience. Inspired by the work of Dr. Lucia Capacchione in *Recovery of Your Inner Child*,[12] using the non-dominant hand to journal, draw, or respond to prompts can be a powerful integration tool. Examples of prompts to access the inner child's needs include asking: "What do you need right now? How are you feeling right now? Do you feel safe right now? How can I support you?" I suggest using a large drawing pad and colorful markers and allowing some time for the writing to start to really flow or revisit the activity often until your inner child feels safe enough to share. Meeting,

---

12 Capacchione, Lucia. Recovery of Your Inner Child: The Highly Acclaimed Method for Liberating Your Inner Self. New York: Simon & Schuster, 1991.

creating safety for, and healing our inner child is a profound and powerful pathway to integration.

The first time I tried this technique was a few years before my first ceremony, as a suggested method to heal my childhood trauma. I was in the process of a very painful divorce, and I was so surprised at the power and force of my inner child's voice and her energy. I had never listened to her before as a separate part within me. What she had to share with me was actually quite comical. "People are not to be trusted, *ever.* I don't need anyone else in my life. Dogs are the only good relationships you can count on...." The more I let her rip the more hysterical her perspective became. She liked the colored pens and large pad to work with. I had the sense that she was quite happy to share all her thoughts on what I needed in my life and how I should move forward. By doing this I was able to realize how readily she lurked beneath the surface of my adult self, waiting for a triggering event so that she could then move into full protection mode. I named her Lizzie and my inner joke continues to be that she prefers to shoot first and ask questions later.

Our Periphery Mind Patterns Are Often Fueled by Core Beliefs

Across many therapeutic and contemplative traditions, from Internal Family Systems to mindfulness-based inquiry, identifying core beliefs is seen as a key to understanding how our protective patterns formed and how healing unfolds. Core beliefs are the deep, often unconscious beliefs we formed in our earliest years—beliefs about ourselves and our place in the world that helped us survive. These beliefs act as gatekeepers for our entire energy system. They originated from our young minds' egocentric attempts to interpret our experiences to support and maintain connection to our caregivers.

From the womb onward, we begin shaping our inner world based on how we are cared for. For example, a baby left to cry in her crib without comfort might internalize the belief that she doesn't matter, that her needs are unimportant. This belief takes root, not just in the mind, but in the body and spirit, and may persist until it is consciously seen and healed. Or consider a toddler raised by a loving but anxious parent who constantly intervenes to prevent danger. That child may come to believe that the world isn't safe, and that she isn't safe in it.

These core beliefs profoundly influence how we perceive and respond to life. They shape the narratives we carry, often reinforcing the patterns of our periphery mind. When we begin to identify and question these beliefs and recognize that they are not true, but rather adaptations from a much younger self, we begin to loosen their grip. This is where real healing begins.

Self-Exploration Exercise: Understanding and Awareness of Our Core Beliefs

This is an exercise to gently reveal the core beliefs that shape your sense of self so they may be understood, reframed and healed. To do this exercise you will need a quiet, comfortable space, your journal, 30 minutes, and an open, curious mindset. You can explore this practice all at one time or break it up into manageable increments. Tune in to see what feels best for your own being.

Begin by choosing a specific situation, relationship, or recurring pat tern in your life that shows up as a big trigger. Example: for me I often feel challenged when I feel disappointed or let down by a friend. Write about it in your journal, "*One area of my life that causes deep reactivity is....*" Example: I really get wound up when my friend doesn't show up in the way I would like.

Now explore what you must believe to be true to cause this trigger and write about it in your journal. "*What must I believe to be true in this situation for me to feel the way I do?*" Example: if my friend lets me down it is because I am not important, people are not trustworthy.... Write whatever comes up without judgment.

Now if it feels right, dig deeper by asking yourself if that belief is true: "What does that mean about me?" Example: I am not safe, I can't rely on friends, I am not important, there is something wrong with me.

Repeat this prompt a few times until you reach a core belief. Example: I am unlovable (or unworthy, or a failure, or I don't matter, or I'm not safe…).

Now, if it feels comfortable, take a moment to reflect on the core belief that emerged. Ask yourself: "Where did I first learn this? Whose voice does this sound like? Is this belief true? How has it affected my life? What might be a more compassionate truth?

Now rewrite the more compassionate truth.
Old belief: *"I am unlovable."*
New understanding: *"I am worthy of love and always have been."*

Integration in body: Lie down on your back in relaxation. Place one hand on your navel center. Breathe slowly into this space. With each breath, silently repeat your new understanding. Feel your center warm and strengthen.

Reflection: "What did I learn about myself through this process? How might this shift how I understand my mind?

Now let's circle back. Look at the image of the sun. It's a miracle that the sun is a star that burns so brightly it lights up our entire solar system. The problem is we think we are the rays and have forgotten we are the star. The sun is within us, our sacred center. Integration is remembering this. By bringing awareness to the rays (our periphery) with gentle attention we then begin to connect with our true selves.

Chapter Thirteen:

Understanding the Mind through the Yogic Lens of Three Bodies

"The Self and the contents of the mind are completely separate."
—Patanjali

The thoughts that we create around our plant medicine experience can aid our integration or hinder it. To understand this let's continue to explore the mind from different perspectives.

The yogis taught that mind is actually three separate bodies, and that each of us has three functional minds: a negative mind, a positive mind, and a neutral mind. The negative and positive minds, when out of balance, live in and fuel our periphery minds.

Negative Mind: Understanding The Protective Voice

The negative mind is important, and its natural job is to protect us from danger. Its role is to help us discern what is supportive versus what is not supportive in our lives. When the negative mind is out of balance, it chatters endlessly about what is wrong in our world and within our being. It actively seeks to reinforce our negative core beliefs because it perceives these beliefs as safeguards. The negative mind's goal is for us to survive and for millennia, human survival has depended on our ability to both perceive threats and to belong and live cooperatively. The negative mind fuels these needs by generating thoughts designed to keep us aligned with the group, so we act in ways that ensure we fit in and thus remain safe.

When the negative mind is out of balance, it does not want you to be an individual. It wants you to blend in with the collective consciousness that surrounds you. And it's important to recognize that it's not just your own negative mind doing this. The negative minds of your family and friends also want you to conform because when you step outside the expected norms, they may feel discomfort. Your transformation can unsettle others because it points to the possibility that change is real and available.

When you understand that the negative mind's ultimate purpose is to help you belong to ensure your survival, you can begin to meet the thoughts it generates with acceptance and compassion, rather than trying to push them away or change them. Just as you would comfort a friend who is feeling low, you can comfort your negative mind by listening, neither identifying with it nor trying to silence it. Bringing awareness to these thoughts and their deeper motivation begins to restore balance.

Watch your thoughts as they arise. Identify negative thoughts, and as you do, try to understand them. Is there a core belief being reinforced here? When you make the choice to become your authentic self, you're essentially signaling to your negative mind that you no longer need to conform to survive and that it no longer needs to perform its original job. This can be unsettling. Meet yourself with compassion as you navigate this process and as you encounter the resistance that inevitably arises. That resistance is fueled by the negative mind. And, as we've explored, resistance is powerful. To meet it, we must apply equal energy in the form of awareness, understanding, and compassion. That's alchemy.

Journal Reflection Prompts: Negative Mind

Before we move further into this chapter, I suggest you spend about ten minutes with your negative mind. Give it free reign. Pull out your journal and free-write all the negative thoughts that arise. Start with the familiar ones such as: *I can't do this, I don't belong, I'm a loser, it's hopeless*. Keep going.

After you are finished, read through them. Are any of them true? How are these thoughts keeping you safe? Reflecting on these questions, spend another ten minutes listing how these thoughts protect you or provide safety. By simply becoming aware of the negative mind patterns and naming them as a separate part of your mind, you can then dis-identify with these thoughts. By disidentifying from them, you disempower them. They are not you.

Becoming an observer is something to play with and practice. The more you do this, the more you will come to realize that negative thoughts are just thoughts, these thoughts are not real or true but rather they are very old energy patterns from the past.

I once had sessions with a client who had a very dark ayahuasca journey. She described how, during the ceremony, it felt as though all the dark, negative thoughts in her mind were on fire with thoughts like *I hate myself, I hate my life, the world is a very bad place*. She was extremely uncomfortable and fought the medicine, trying desperately to escape the loop of her mind. But when the ceremony ended, the energy of the negative mind continued unabated. This was deeply disconcerting for her, especially because she presented herself outwardly as an easygoing, happy person.

It was my understanding that the medicine had acted as a mirror, revealing the unconscious shadow just beneath the surface, perhaps explaining why, despite her cheerful exterior, she was often short-fused and lacked empathy. Through our integration work, she came to understand that the medicine had shown her the hidden inner thoughts and beliefs she hadn't known were there, but which had been influencing her every move. This is an example of how, when the negative mind is out of balance and suppressed as something bad, its dark energy stagnates within us. What it truly needs is healthy acknowledgment and compassionate release.

Positive Mind: The Expansive Voice Within

The positive mind is also hard at work keeping us safe. Like the negative mind, it too needs to be in balance. Your positive mind manifests as the risk taker, the party goer, the one who won't take no for an answer. It wants to be seen and recognized. This is the part of you that tries to view the world through rose-colored lenses. When we minimize or deny our pain and suffering, this is the positive mind out of balance. Minimizing our life experience is another way to block energy and also block healing. While the positive mind insists everything is just fine, our unacknowledged pain takes root in the body and can manifest as disease or illness. In our society, we often encourage positivity as more desirable, so we create a false positive persona and expend our life energy to shut down pain and maintain the mask. When our positive minds are out of balance, we deprive ourselves of authentic life experience. We lose the depth and receptivity that support growth, healing, and maturity.

Identify your positive mind and explore how it helps and how it hinders you. By becoming conscious of this mind, you begin to bring it into balance. If you have a weak positive mind, you can strengthen it through the cultivation of gratitude and optimism by choosing to see potential and growth while staying grounded in your own experience, your felt sense, and your navel. Practices like gratitude journaling and affirmations can help retrain the positive mind to balance the negative mind without trying to suppress it. A balanced positive mind doesn't deny difficulty or pain. It meets these with courage, creativity, and the understanding that authentic positivity is rooted in honesty with self.

Positive Mind and the Quicksand That Is Spiritual Bypassing

In terms of sacred plant medicine, the positive mind is where spiritual bypassing happens. Spiritual bypassing is a term used to describe the tendency to use spiritual ideas or practices to avoid facing unresolved emotional issues, psychological wounds, or uncomfortable realities. It often masquerades as having arrived somewhere, but beneath the surface it denies pain, bypasses grief, and suppresses truth in favor of a more esteemed spiritual identity. Statements like, "I've healed my childhood trauma, I am ready to serve medicine or teach" can become detrimental when used to avoid the real work of healing.

The positive mind invites us to skip the painful process of healing with the idea that we have arrived and are healed. This is very common and very sad, as people miss true healing by buying into this defensive energetic quicksand. Spiritual bypassing can also negatively impact those misled by the person's positive projection. For the spiritual bypasser now bent on becoming a shaman, the positive mind is the one leading the charge to teach and serve with adopted knowledge, rather than waiting to be invited into such a role due to true depth and wisdom.

The positive mind, when healthy and balanced, does indeed give us the capacity to see opportunity, potential, and growth and can be supportive during challenging times. It reflects the aspect of consciousness that says, "I can do this, there is something to learn here." The balanced positive mind supports expansion and the will to act. When out of balance or disconnected from grounding and discernment, it can be tempted to slip into spiritual bypassing to avoid pain.

In integration work, especially after profound plant medicine experiences, the risk of bypassing is real. The medicine may reveal light and unity, but it also often brings up shadow, trauma, and old conditionings. The positive mind alone is not enough to integrate these experiences. We need the presence of the neutral mind, the space of witnessing and acceptance, as well as the grounding of the negative mind, which helps us see potential risks and patterns that need healing.

True healing includes discomfort. It asks us to be courageous enough to witness our pain without spiritualizing it away. Integration is not about staying positive; it is about becoming whole. That means holding space for all parts of our experience and the polarities that are inherent within us, such as joy and grief, light and shadow, with compassion, honesty, and humility.

Neutral Mind: The Inner Witness

As we explored in the last chapter, the subtle neutral mind of the yogis is the sun, the center of our mind, with the rays serving as the periphery. In connection with the navel, the neutral mind is the sacred center of you. Your subtle neutral mind must be cultivated for integration to truly take root; this requires the navel energy to be open and in flow as these centers are energetically connected. Your neutral mind is your nonreactive, responsive self. It lives in the present. This is your meditative mind. This is the mind that supports, encourages, and allows space for integration to flourish in your being. Strengthening your neutral mind is key to your evolution and change. Coming from a place of neutrality and responsiveness rather than reactivity creates freedom. By balancing the polarities of the negative and positive minds, you can begin to connect to the neutral mind and recognize that the rays emanating from each polarity are not you. Our goal in the process of integration is to be rooted in the navel and to be aware and act from neutral mind. This is freedom.

Before we explore the mind further, let's take a moment to summarize the aspects of the mind that we've explored so far. It's important to understand how the mind works in the context of integration. Your preferences are at play: your ideas of what is good or bad are your mind's way of trying to label and create meaning, even where meaning may not be required. This is an invitation to let go of preferences and simply be with what is, without labeling.

Your periphery mind is trying to interpret, protect, define, and contain your experience. No need to resist, just bring awareness to this energy within. Your positive and negative minds are each working to make sense of the journey, while your neutral mind stands by in nonjudgment, waiting to help you go deeper. If you simply view your medicine ceremony as positive, you may miss the subtle healing available in the shadow. Likewise, if your experience was dark, the negative mind may define it as a bad trip, and you could miss what lies beneath. For example, if you were caught in a womb of darkness and fear during your ceremony, and your negative mind interprets this as bad or unhelpful, you may miss the opportunity to understand and heal a subtle layer of separation, disconnection, or dark energy that you carry within.

Chapter Fourteen:

The Multi-Layered Mind on the Integration Path

"All that we are is the result of what we have thought. The mind is everything. What we think, we become."
—The Buddha, The Dhammapada, Verse 1

In this chapter I provide an overview of the psychology of the layers of mind (conscious, subconscious, and unconscious) from a laywoman's perspective. I offer this as a way for you to understand how your mind is a fertile field for integration and to better grasp what that looks like on a practical level.

When we work with hauchuma in the Andes we begin our ceremony before the sun sets by lighting a sacred fire that we attune to throughout the night. We sit in meditation and prayer with the sacred medicine until the sun rises, guided by our maestro's songs and our own songs of remembrance and gratitude. Sometimes, just before the sun rises our maestro tells us stories of the lineage there, and there is space for laughter and questions. On one such early morning, our guide spoke of three worlds, and I transcribed his teachings in my journal. I can picture myself resting in my tent after the ceremony: hot, sweaty, covered in insect bites, writing about these three worlds. He described an underworld, a middle world, and an upper world, in which the Inca nobles were able to travel to create harmony with the help of sacred plant medicine. As I reread my scribbled notes to write about the chakana, I realized that these three worlds are also a metaphor for the layers of the human mind. Each of the chakana's four sides carries three symbolic steps, representing these three worlds, leading toward the Four Directions, a reminder that wherever we turn, our journey moves through all realms of existence. Indeed, the three worlds of Andean cosmology, which predate modern psychology by thousands of years, also offer a layered map of the mind.

In *Ukhu Pacha*, which my guide called the underworld, we meet the unconscious mind through memory, dream, and shadow. In *Kay Pacha*, described as the middle world, the mind lives in action, our daily conscious thoughts that make up our world. In *Hanan Pacha*, described as the upper world, we connect with our subtle, neutral mind through acceptance, let go, and presence.

Modern psychology mirrors these ancient understandings. Another way to work with the mind in your integration process is to explore the conscious, subconscious, and unconscious minds, as originally described by Freud. The conscious mind is the surface mind, the stream of thoughts we hear in our heads as we go about our day. These thoughts are powerful and shape our realities. This is the mind that constructs and upholds our ego identities and narratives. I often refer to it as the cognitive mind, as its role is cognition in the realm of the material world.

The cognitive mind wants to create a narrative around your plant medicine journey that feels manageable and complete. But these experiences are not linear, they unfold mysteriously, beyond the mind's grasp. The mind, uncomfortable with ambiguity, tries to fill in the gaps with assumptions, false beliefs, or stories that may soothe short-term discomfort but limit long-term insight. If we allow the mind to define the journey too quickly, we may miss the deeper layers still in motion.

Beneath the conscious mind lies the subconscious mind, a memory bank. It stores information that arises when needed. For example, when I recently struggled to recall a woman's name during a conversation, it resurfaced hours later on its own. That's the subconscious at work. In your integration, you may recall forgotten moments, memories, or meanings that resurface when the time is right.

My own experience of being with my grandmother Effie in my first ceremony, for example, was a healing of a subconscious memory. I had carried the guilt and grief of not saying goodbye to her, buried so deeply I didn't realize it was still there. The ceremony brought it to the surface and transformed it.

Even more vital to integration is the unconscious mind. This is the vast, deep reservoir where repressed memories, instincts, and unresolved emotions live. Though hidden, these forces influence our behaviors and beliefs every day. Beneath our thoughts and memories are countless impressions from childhood which are unseen but shaping us, like the moon shapes the ocean's tides. These unconscious layers feed our periphery mind and color how we interpret and respond to life. The yogis teach that the troubled unconscious mind is the root of all disease: mental, emotional, and physical. The work, then, is to meet this layer and bring light to what lies there.

We do this not through *willpower* but through building and expanding our subtle, neutral mind. This allows us to hold the *mesa* (sacred altar) of our lives with presence and awareness. Holding the mesa of our lives means moving in sacred presence more and more. Presence requires our being connected and centered to ourselves. We connect to ourselves and feel centered only through the subtle mind.

As we explored in Chapter Three, we also carry the collective unconscious, a term introduced by Carl Jung. This is a shared well of archetypes, dreams, and symbols passed through generations, present in all human psyches. It lives beneath the personal unconscious and connects us to a deeper lineage of meaning and myth. In integration, tapping into the collective unconscious can help us recognize archetypal patterns in our own healing journey: the wounded healer, the descent and return, as well as the sacred union of opposites. These reveal that our personal healing is also part of a much greater story.

When we journey with sacred medicines, we often go beyond the conscious mind into the unconscious and collective unconscious realms. A core part of integration is becoming aware of what surfaced there, what messages, wounds, or truths were revealed in those deeper waters. Through conscious reflection, journaling, inquiry, and meditation, we begin to translate those messages into our daily lives. Awareness brings understanding, and understanding brings release. What once lived hidden in the dark can become a source of strength, clarity, and transformation.

For example, I understand now that my unconscious longing for a true mother was met in that first ceremony when I laid upon Pachamama and cried. The Earth received my tears, not as grief alone but as prayers. That moment was a remembrance, a reconciliation, and a turning point. A healing that began in the unconscious became embodied through integration.

Journal Reflection Prompts: Explore the Conscious, Subconscious, and Unconscious Mind

Let's explore these layers of mind through self-reflective journaling. Spend some time exploring the following prompts as they relate to your integration.

Conscious Mind: What am I currently focused on in my personal healing or growth? Why?

Subconscious Mind: What memories or impressions from my past are being stirred or reawakened as I integrate my plant medicine journey? How might these be asking for attention, healing, or understanding now?

Unconscious Mind: What and how do I sense my unconscious mind working in my integration and in my life right now? What aspects, if any, seem to be connected to the collective unconscious mind?

Back to the Sacred Center: The Subtle Mind

Throughout our exploration of the mind, I've referred often to the subtle neutral mind. This mind resides at the center of the chakana, chawpin. In Sanskrit, this quality of mind is called *suka*. The yoga posture sukhasana is named after this state of being. Ease, joy, good energy, fluidity, and contentment are all qualities of the subtle mind. This is our natural state, mirroring the rhythms and harmony of nature itself. Suka lives dormant within us and can be cultivated by bringing awareness to our periphery and unconscious patterns. When we do this, we begin to regulate our internal energy flow regardless of external circumstances.

Accessing suka expands our capacity to hold stress and navigate life's challenges; it becomes a kind of inner shield. Our resilience lives here. When we live from this place, a quiet alchemy occurs. We begin responding to life, rather than reacting. Our responses are born of presence, compassion, and love. This subtle mind is the essential you. It is the part of you that you may have touched in ceremony, and when you remember it, you reconnect with the nucleus of your being, which is love.

Spiraling back to the polarities within us, suka has a counterpart, *duka*. Duka is *dis-ease*, energetic imbalance, and the mind in conflict. It's the state of being out of alignment with the subtle mind, caught instead in the material plane, ruled by the periphery, disconnected from our senses. But duka is not something to fight. Resistance only fuels it. When we meet it with attention, with respect, when we greet it as we would a sacred guest in ceremony, we create the alchemy that reveals the path back to suka.

The conscious thoughts you're having about your experience are not isolated. They're deeply influenced by subconscious memories and early life patterns that shaped your way of being. Your meaning-making mind is woven with unconscious beliefs from childhood, shaped in the effort to survive. These personal layers, along with the collective unconscious, swirl beneath the surface of your integration. The unconscious knows no bounds: it moves through archetypes, memory, and myth fluidly.

Our task is not to control the mind, but to become aware of these layers and bring them into balance. When we do, our subtle mind becomes the conductor, and our energy flows. This is suka. This is integration.

Clarity: Reclaiming Harmony Within the Mind

In these chapters, we've invited the mind into your sacred circle as a guest in the ceremony that is your life. We've explored the mind through many lenses. My intention has been to help you understand how the mind moves, both during ceremony and in the ongoing ceremony of daily life.

We each carry a subtle, neutral mind that mirrors the sun itself: radiant, centered, aware. This is the balancing force in our beings, the heart of the chakana, and the mind we are learning to remember. On the periphery, we carry all the aspects of mind that we are not: preferences, beliefs, the positive and negative minds, ego identities, unconscious, and protective parts. These are important, but they are not meant to oversee our integration. When they do, we suffer.

Through awareness, we begin to alchemize the mind's chatter. We reframe. We revisit. We ask where a thought came from. We apply compassion. This is all that is required. Learning to witness the mind without *identifying as it* is a lifelong, even multi-lifetime process. But this witnessing—this separation—is the essence of meditation. It is the medicine.

Meditation is witnessing the mind. Each time we notice a thought and recognize it as just a thought, we step closer to our sun center, chawpin. We move closer to integration, to inner alchemy, where life itself becomes the ceremony. With awareness, with compassion, with presence, we meet the periphery and return to wholeness. This is the sacred path of self-study. One breath, one step at a time.

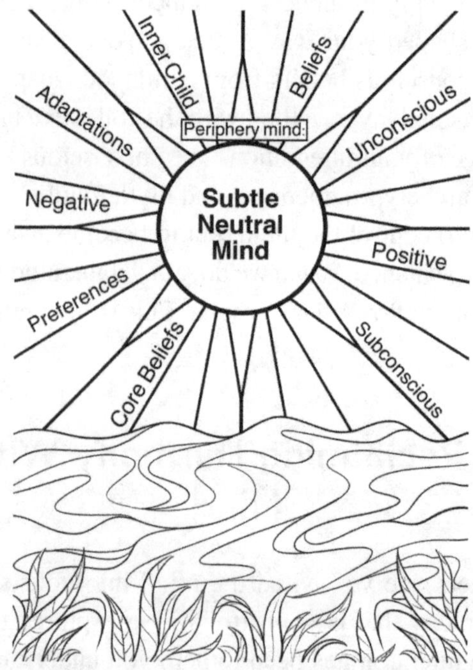

When we start to witness our periphery mind by meeting it with compassion and kindness rather than judgment, we are able to then connect to our more subtle neutral mind.

Self-Exploration Exercise: Gibberish

As we have explored, everything is energy and energy needs to move. A powerful meditation technique to work with the mind is gibberish. Speaking gibberish is an opportunity to allow the mind to throw out its frenetic energy without real language: to apply some friction, and to receive in return relief from the flood of thoughts that comprises our periphery minds.

The contemporary mystic, Osho, introduced gibberish as a powerful tool to bypass the controlling, analytical mind. He taught that by speaking in nonsense syllables and sounds, one can express repressed thoughts and emotions, break through inner rigidity, and enter into a state of spacious presence. For Osho, gibberish was a way to throw out the mental noise and allow the witness to emerge.

Osho's No Mind (Gibberish) Meditation includes two stages. The first involves speaking complete nonsense, while allowing the body and voice to move freely without meaning or structure. This stage is deliberately cathartic and chaotic, intended to release the grip of rational thought. The second stage is silent witnessing. After the outpouring of gibberish, the meditator is invited to sit in stillness and observe whatever arises. In essence, we throw out our periphery mind, our positive and negative minds, our subconscious and unconscious minds, to then connect to our subtle neutral mind.

We offer a seven-day No Mind Intensive every spring at the Leela Foundation, a nonprofit meditation center I help run in Boulder, as a way to release stagnant energy and greet spring with a fresh clear mind set. We call it a spring cleaning and I have found that it really works on all levels.

The gibberish technique has found its way into other therapeutic and spiritual modalities. It is used in expressive arts therapy, trauma-informed therapy, voice work, etc. I personally have used it in my sacred plant medicine integration; I have found it is a powerful tool for my clients, as well. Though it may seem strange or uncomfortable at first, gibberish invites play, surrender, and a kind of sacred absurdity. It challenges the seriousness of the ego and opens a portal to creativity and intuition. In a culture dominated by our mind center, gibberish offers a rare opportunity to let go of control and rediscover the freedom of simply being.

Instructions: Find a quiet place where you can move freely and make noise. Loud drumming music or other similar music can be played to support this process. Set your timer for 11- 20 minutes and just start making gibberish noises. Baby talk, nonsense words, duh, duh, duh, just throw out sounds in a language that you do not know. Follow your body's lead as you gibber away. Be totally present in this—really go for it—and allow any emotions that arise to move through, but don't stop making the sounds. This is a way to literally allow the mind to release energy from within. After the time is up sit down in a relaxed posture and meditate for at least ten minutes. Doing seven days of gibberish is an amazing reset for the mind. Your mind might be saying, "Well that doesn't make sense, how could that help?" I can tell you from years of practice that this is a powerful tool to balance the energies of the mind.

Chapter Fifteen:

Emotional Depth in Integration

"Water does not resist. Water flows. When you plunge your hand into it, all you feel is a caress. Water is not a solid wall, it will not stop you. But water always goes where it wants to go, and nothing in the end can stand against it. Water is patient. Dripping water wears away a stone. Remember that, my child. Remember you are half water. If you can't go through an obstacle, go around it. Water does."

—Margaret Atwood

In the last chapters, we explored the mind center, our thoughts, their patterns, and how their energies shape our lives. I invited you to begin the process of disidentifying from the mind: to notice your habitual thoughts, preferences, and identifications that construct your outer identity, and to bring awareness to them so their deeper origins can begin to heal from within. This was an invitation to move from outer constructions created by the mind toward the inner work that lives beyond it.

Now we turn to the third energy center to nurture in our integration process: the emotional center, the heart. This is a precious guest in our ceremonial circle. Our emotional center plays a vital role in integration. Understanding how our emotions influence this journey can open the door to deeper meaning, fuller healing, and greater embodiment.

Our Heart Centers Want to Flow

Let's explore emotions. The emotional center in the body is the heart. In both the Chakana and Eastern teachings, it is symbolized by the water element and indeed, our emotions are like water. Water can flow strongly, trickle, stagnate, be still, or appear cloudy, muddy, or clear. We want our internal waters, our emotions, to flow like sacred rivers toward the ocean, to be released into the whole and let go.

What are emotions? Emotions are feelings. They arise in the heart center. They are not of the mind, they are of the body. We do not think from our hearts, we feel. There is an intelligence and energy at the heart center, our emotional center, that is not governed by the mind, but we have lost our connection to it.

When we experience emotions, typically a feeling comes first, and then the mind jumps in to interpret it. Let's look at how this unfolds within us. Let's say we see an old friend from a distance. We remember a painful event from the past. Before any thought arises in the conscious mind, we feel an emotion, perhaps sadness. That's the initial, raw feeling in the heart. Then the mind begins to create a short narrative, a perception, something like, "I was rejected by that friend." That perception then gets interpreted: "This was so terrible. It ruined my life." Then the mental loop takes over: "I should have said something. I wish I could go back and change that..."

When we move from the initial feeling of sadness to the perception of rejection, we disconnect from the heart and rise into the mind. We leave the emotional body and move into the mind's interpretation. Each time we do this, we bypass the raw emotion and lose an opportunity to be present and heal. We carry our wounds in our bodies because we have lost contact with the ability to stay present in the heart.

In my guiding work, I often invite people to pause and sense what lives beneath the words—the feeling that gives the story its charge. Often, the initial response is not a true emotion, but a perception of that emotion. For example, a client might say, "I felt helpless. I couldn't ask for support." Helplessness, while valid, is a mental overlay. I guide them gently to the feeling beneath helplessness. Often, it's fear. But the client's experience of fear was never expressed. It remained hidden and unacknowledged in the heart center. Instead, the mind reinforced the belief of helplessness.

To heal the mind's core belief—for example, "I'm helpless"—we must feel the feeling that formed it. When a feeling is avoided or dismissed, it stagnates. The more we avoid it, the more the heart closes, and the stronger the periphery mind becomes. This often leads to mental looping, a repetitive inner narrative that plays on repeat. The looping mind becomes a defense mechanism to avoid feeling what the heart is still holding.

Integration requires that we access and metabolize our emotions.

Sacred plant medicine is a powerful healing modality. In ceremony, we are often shown our wounds without a mental narrative to explain them. That is part of healing. The invitation is to meet the emotion, not just the interpretation of the experience, to drop beneath the mental story and connect with the heart. When we can do that, we transform. We become present. We heal.

This is the integration journey—from the head to the heart.

Why We Need to Reopen Our Heart Centers

We are conditioned from an early age to believe that many of our natural emotions are bad, and as a result, we learn to censor them. Anger, pride, hatred, jealousy, excitement, enthusiasm are often condemned or shamed by our caregivers. The problem with this is that when we shut these emotions down, when we stifle them, we also lose connection to their opposites and to our hearts. This is where the masks we explored in the last chapter are truly created. When we suppress our true feelings, we also suppress our authenticity.

Moreover, the emotions we are taught to hide are often the ones that empower us. Anger, for example, is a potent energy that can connect us directly to our navel center, our fire element, and our source of will, determination, and courage.

These suppressed emotions don't disappear. They remain within us, unexpressed, and instead of being metabolized, they begin to feed the periphery mind. They actively fuel the looping thoughts and reactive patterns of the mind. Rather than repressing them, we are invited to alchemize them within the heart center.

Remember, everything is energy. Emotions are fluid energy moving through us. And just like thoughts, they exist along a spectrum of polarities with which we can consciously engage. Our feelings are not isolated; they are interconnected by the same life force. There is a flow between the polarities within us: the energy that feeds hate also fuels love; the energy that fuels pride also feeds humility; jealousy shares a root with admiration and respect; anger transforms into passion, and ultimately into compassion.

When we suppress one side of a polarity because we've been conditioned to believe it is unacceptable, we simultaneously block its opposite. We might feel safe or controlled, but we also feel flat, disconnected, or numb. We've been taught that some emotions make us good and others make us bad and in doing so, we've lost access to the fullness of our heart center and our ability to truly feel.

Only through honest, embodied expression can emotions be transformed. In their natural state, emotions, like all energy, are neutral. If we allow that energy to move, it brings us back into balance. This is integration. We reconnect to our hearts by bringing awareness and acceptance to whatever is there, rather than suppressing or avoiding it. It's painful to sit with the darker emotions, but when we do, they alchemize. On the other side of that alchemy lies access to the more life-giving qualities, such as love, respect, humility, passion, compassion.

On another level, the unprocessed emotional pain from childhood is still held in the body, waiting to be felt and released. Healing can only happen through feeling. When we were children, we were often taught to suppress our emotions in order to survive, to belong, to avoid rejection. But those emotions didn't vanish. They were pushed down into the body and the unconscious mind, where they continue to live and influence us.

We spend our vital life-force energy holding them down.

That energy, once used to guard against pain, grief, rage, or shame, is no longer available for creativity, growth, joy, and presence. Integration invites us to reclaim that energy by gently bringing awareness to what's been suppressed within and allowing it to move again.

Understanding That Perceptions Are Not Feelings

To move towards the wholeness that is integration, it's helpful to express and honor our emotions rather than hide from them or allow them to unconsciously direct our lives. All the energies of the heart center are worthy of exploration, with curiosity, not judgment. A good first step is to begin noticing the difference between perceptions and feelings.

Perceptions, as we explored above, are interpretations of feelings. They are movements from the heart center up into the mind. Statements like: "I feel rejected, I feel disrespected, I feel betrayed, I feel unwanted, I feel lonely, I feel unsafe" are not pure feelings; they are perceptions layered over emotional experiences. What are the core feelings that lie beneath them?

The basic emotions of anger, excitement, sadness, disgust, joy, fear, each have a natural function and energetic signature when in flow. Let's look at them more closely:

- Anger arises to assert, fight, or defend. In its natural state, it is empowering and activates the will.
- Excitement propels us toward the new. It sparks curiosity, movement, and exploration.
- Sadness signals a need for support. It shows us what is meaningful, what we love, and what we've lost.
- Disgust originally protected us from ingesting harmful substances. Over time, it has evolved to include intuitive boundaries around what feels toxic or unsafe.
- Joy opens the heart and helps us thrive through connection and sharing.
- Fear protects us. Its natural role is to alert us to threats and help us move toward protection.
- Sexual desire and its accompanying excitement began as a means of ensuring survival through reproduction. Now, it also supports connection, fulfillment, and the experience of embodied pleasure.

Each of these emotions arises in the body and creates a physiological and energetic pattern that impacts our whole being. When in balance and flow, these energies support our innate wisdom. Emotion is energy in motion and integration requires that we allow this energy to move. The medicine journey often mirrors back what is unresolved or stuck. The invitation is to see clearly, to feel deeply, and to allow that energy to complete its natural cycle.

So, we begin by identifying the perception that may be blocking the emotion. These mind constructs dampen or divert the flow of feeling. If we can gently move beneath the perception to the raw emotion itself and give that emotion space, we begin to heal. Sit with the feeling. Meditate on it. Name it. Let it be seen. In doing so, we release it and reclaim the life energy that had been used to suppress it.

For example: "What is this? Sadness. How do I know it's sadness? What does it feel like in my body?"

The goal is not to fix the emotion, but to *feel* it. When we begin to befriend our emotions, self-understanding deepens. Our emotional fluidity returns. Balance arises. Authenticity becomes more natural. Alchemy unfolds.

Journal Reflection Prompts: Perception vs. Feeling

This is an exercise to help us reconnect with the emotions that get lost beneath our perceptions.

Start by thinking of a recent interaction that was uncomfortable and then see if you can name a perception that came up. Take a breath. Choose one word that best describes the perception (rejected, disrespected, disempowered, abandoned, unwanted, etc.)

"I feel __________."
Example: I feel rejected

Take a breath. Notice what you're feeling right now. Choose one word from the list of emotions above that best describes the emotion beneath the perception.

"I feel __________."
Example: I feel sad

This exercise helps uncover how the mind can label, judge, or interpret emotions, robbing us of our authentic need and capacity to feel them in real time. As soon as we label, judge or interpret our experience, we have moved from feeling the emotion and being present with it into the periphery mind. Integration begins when we learn to separate the narrative from the experience itself.

Befriending Fear

One of the most common themes in plant medicine journeys is fear—before, during, and after ceremony. Learning how to relate to fear is essential. Rather than resisting or avoiding it, we bring awareness to it. We name it: "This is fear." We breathe into it. We speak to it with compassion: "Yes, I see you. I feel you in my belly. You are here to warn me, to protect me. Thank you."

When we can treat fear as an ally, it softens. It relaxes within us instead of contracting. If, however, we shut fear down, we also shut down our ability to surrender to the medicine and its healing intelligence. Surrender and breath are essential. When we can relax into the fear and allow it to crest like a wave, we often find ourselves on the other side in a place of calm, presence, and clarity, like the tide receding back into the sea.

This process is as much a part of integration as it is during the ceremony itself.

Fear is the doorway that we must pass through for healing, growth, and expansion. Making it an ally is essential. Feeling it, recognizing it, honoring it, and not letting it keep us small and taking us off our healing paths is the heavy lifting that brings us home to ourselves.

Other Ways to Bring Awareness to Our Emotional Energies

Naming

Another way to access and work with emotions is to treat the process like a naming ceremony. As emotions arise, name them. Think of your avoided or forbidden emotions as trapped waters, energies dammed up by the mind in an effort to avoid feeling them. When you name them, you give them permission to flow again. Naming becomes an act of reverence, a sacred release.

By blocking emotion, we create murky, stagnant pools in our hearts. As we name what arises, those waters begin to move again becoming clearer, flowing like rivers toward the sea. When we honor emotion in this way, we understand that pain and suffering are not fixed but fluid, and flow naturally if allowed. This opens the doorway to compassion, not just for ourselves but for all humanity. We realize that our emotions are not ours alone; they are part of the whole.

This recognition becomes a critical gateway. When we allow ourselves to feel our very real, very human pain, we reconnect to the heart center and that is where true healing happens. So, as emotions arise, we say: *Ah, this is sadness. Ah, this is anger. Ah, this is joy.* And we hold each one with reverence until it releases in its own time.

Triggers

Another valuable tool I use, both in my own practice and with clients, is working with emotional triggers. Through years of somatic and inquiry-based study, I've learned to recognize these moments of activation as invitations to look deeper. A trigger is a present-moment spark that awakens an old emotion still seeking resolution. When this happens, the periphery mind is strongly activated. Every mental defense we've developed rushes forward to protect us, often creating internal or external chaos.

Our inner child and the wounds that she experienced are often at the core of our triggers. For example, I have a deep inner child wound related to women. When this wound is activated in an interaction with a friend, the interaction loses its present context and becomes entangled with a much older drama. I am no longer the adult me in relationship with a friend. I am responding from the child who was once deeply hurt, defending herself against that same old pain.

To come back to myself, I pause and inquire: *What is the feeling I'm protecting? Where does it live in my body? How long has it been there?* This process doesn't always bring instant relief, but it helps me re-regulate. The more I do this, the less reactive my triggers become. This is healing.

When we allow space to feel the emotions that arise after our journey, we drop into the heart center and move out of the mind center. This is good medicine.

I was reminded of this deeply in a ceremony last year in the jungle. I found myself face to face with the grief of my inner child. It was piercing. I heard a small, young voice within me say: "I miss my daddy." The pain was so sharp, so immediate, that all I could do was breathe and let the silent tears flow. After the ceremony, the grief lingered. It was raw, powerful, and I had to sit with it over the days that followed.

Even now, as I write this, I feel that sadness. The story of why I miss my father is deeply personal, but the *feeling* of missing him, of grieving the loss of his presence in my life, had been buried since I was about five years old. I had tucked it away, hidden it. But in ceremony, it came back with full force. It was nearly unbearable. Riding that wave felt like the journey of many lifetimes.

And yet, on the other side of that wave, I felt a tremendous energy shift, an exquisite beauty. Gratitude welled up in me. Gratitude for my life. For my father, who gave me life. For the gift of love and grief.

This is the alchemy of emotional integration. Polarities held in the heart. The wave of grief, when fully met, became a current of love and joy. Grief transformed into gratitude. Emotion in motion. Fluid. Like water.

Journal Reflection Prompts: Explore Your Emotions

I provide a few prompts to help you explore your emotional center below. Free writing on your emotions and how you experience them can also be very supportive as an ongoing exercise in self care.

What are you feeling about your journey now?

What feelings were present before your journey.

What emotions did you experience during your journey?

What emotions are here now in your integration?

If you can identify your actual feelings, you are ahead of the game. If you're not sure, see if you can find the perception, such as "I feel lonely" and then identify the emotion underneath (sad). Circling back to the felt sense practice is helpful if this is challenging for you. We are shut off from our emotional bodies and our hearts are closed to protect us from pain. Integration is about opening the heart to feel the emotion. We feel our pain, and this allows us to feel empathy for others' pain. This is how we develop genuine compassion.

Let's circle back to the navel. By accessing the navel, we lift and open our hearts. The physical posture of having our hearts lifted is a posture that serves as a remembrance to lead with the heart. To lead with the heart, the energy channels to that center must be open. To have the energy channels open, we must remove the dam that blocks the flow of energy, open it up.

To open it up we must feel the feelings. If we try to process our emotions in the mind, we identify. If we process the emotions in the body, we heal.

I am aware that for many people, accessing emotions, especially the deeper, more vulnerable ones, can be profoundly difficult. This isn't because the emotions aren't there, but because they are blocked. And they have been blocked because we had to block them to survive as children, to function, belong, and stay safe. These blocks cause us to disconnect from ourselves. Over time, this creates an internal divide where emotions still operate beneath the surface, but we lose fluency in how to name, feel, or express them. This causes us to feel disconnected from ourselves and from the world.

Emotions are inherently of the body, not of the mind. Yet many of us live primarily in the mind, thinking our perceptions are true feelings. This makes emotional access challenging, especially after intense or sacred experiences like plant medicine ceremonies, which can open floodgates of sensation and memory. Without tools, you may freeze, numb out, or default to familiar defenses.

Think baby steps. Don't overload your system. With practice and self-compassion, emotional awareness can be remembered. Reconnecting to what we feel is a core part of healing and integration. Feeling our feelings allows us to be more embodied and relaxes the energy that feeds the periphery mind, which can then flow toward our more neutral presence.

Connecting with your five senses, practicing the felt sense, practicing long, slow, deep breathing, and walking proud by keeping the heart lifted can all support this process.

Explore Active Meditation: Humming Meditation

Another beautiful meditation technique that can support the heart is humming. Sit in sukhasana with eyes closed and hum out loud for 11 minutes. Allow the vibration of the sound to move up and down your spine like a hollow bamboo. Feel it start at your navel and rise up your energy centers as you inhale through the nose and vibrate the humming sound. Playing music such as Tibetan bowls or gentle sounds of nature will support this.

If humming resonates with you and you want to go deeper, I highly recommend the hour-long Osho Nadabrahma Meditation, which includes humming followed by gentle hand mudras of giving and receiving. I have offered this meditation weekly over the years and continue to practice it myself, particularly when navigating grief. You can find it on streaming platforms. This is a beautiful meditation that ends in deep relaxation and evokes healing in a gentle and profound way.

> *"By humming and hand movements you bring the conflicting parts of you in tune with each other and bring harmony to your whole being. Then, with body and mind totally together, you "slip out of their hold" and become a witness to both. This witnessing from the outside is what brings peace, silence and bliss."*
>
> —Osho

Part Three: Our Ceremony Unfolds

"Like a boundless sea, we have the capacity to embrace the waves of life as they move through us. Even when the sea is stirred up by the winds of self-doubt, we can find our way home. We can discover in the midst of the waves our spacious and wakeful awareness."

—Tara Brach

Chapter Sixteen:

Embodied Awareness

Having the courage to participate in a sacred medicine ceremony is a testament to all the healing work we have done in this lifetime and previous lifetimes. Ultimately, sacred plant medicine ceremonies focus on healing the body, mind, emotions, and spirit. Bringing the previous chapters together, we circle back now to the traditional intentions for this work of healing and self-knowledge that we explored in Chapter Two. Our prayer or intention is to heal ourselves, our loved ones, our fellow humans, Pachamama, and to become more aware and more present so that we can experience life directly, so that our lives can be a ceremony.

As you seek to integrate, your mind might be dancing with questions. How can I heal this wound? I know it's there. How can I change this habit, this pattern in my life that creates such suffering? I experienced healing on my journey when I was purging, what was that about? In the ceremony I felt pain in my chest, grief in my lungs, burning in my throat, why? Now that your back to your ordinary state of consciousness the sensations are gone, but the memory and experience of them are present with you. To answer these questions becomes an end goal for the mind and creates internal strife that is not necessary. There are no answers is a koan for you to consider and dance with for these kinds of thoughts.

> *"Your conflicts, all the difficult things, the problematic situations in your life, are not chance or haphazard. They are actually yours. They are specifically yours, designed specifically for you by a part of you that loves you more than anything else."*
>
> —A.H. Almaas

My Own Healing Journey

My journey of healing has been an arduous and sacred adventure. It began with a childhood that lacked the love, safety, and stability every child needs. My mother abandoned me at the age of four, just as I was beginning kindergarten. I believe my father, a young man himself, did his best as a single parent and eventually remarried when I was seven. His new wife, a woman shaped by her own pain, brought an atmosphere of control, manipulation, and emotional violence into our home.

She isolated our family from extended relatives, including my beloved grandmother Effie, who had been one of my only sources of warmth and connection. I became the scapegoat for her insecurity, jealousy, and resentment. In the shadow of her presence, I experienced emotional abuse that cut deep into my core. I was also sexually abused in my childhood. As a result, I internalized the belief that I was unlovable and unsafe, not as a thought, but as a living truth etched into the tissues of my body.

For years, I tried to outrun that truth by achieving. I earned degrees, held leadership roles, accomplished milestones, all in an unconscious attempt to prove my worth. But no amount of external success could fill the hollow ache within. Despite years of traditional therapy where I received lots of sympathy for my terrible childhood, it wasn't until my late thirties that I truly began my healing journey, when I took responsibility for this pain as my own healing path rather than something bad that had happened to me.

At first, the idea that I had chosen this life—this particular constellation of parents and experiences was difficult to accept. The question "Why did I choose these parents?" became a koan that I worked with that helped me to step on to a more empowered path for myself. Over time, that understanding, rooted in self-responsibility became one of the greatest keys to my healing. Seeing my early suffering through the lens of my spiritual journey allowed me to find meaning in the pain. The depth of despair I once carried has given rise to the depth of my compassion. The aching emptiness became the wellspring of my empathy. And for that, I am deeply grateful.

I understand that my parents are not bad people. They are on their own journeys and may have gotten lost along the way. I have deep compassion and pray for their own healing, and I respect the freedom that they each have to live their lives and learn the lessons they are here to experience. My mom and I are quite close now and healing that relationship has been one of the most sacred milestones on my path home to myself. It has not been easy, but I have learned so much about myself through this process. Forgiveness is not about the other person in the relationship, it is an internal process of letting go of *what is not* and accepting *what is* without judgment, but rather with compassion. Knowing that the pain I experienced in my childhood is a part of a lineage of pain handed down through the generations gives a perspective that allows for healing and growth, rather than victimhood and bitterness. I take it on as my own responsibility at the same time understanding that it is not personal to me. Humbling.

Sacred plant medicines have played a powerful role in my healing, helping me to face the shadows, release old wounds, and receive profound insights. But the real work, the lasting healing, has happened slowly, steadily, in the quiet space of integration. It's happened in the daily practice of meeting the parts of myself we've explored in the last chapters, my own integration ceremony guests of navel, mind, and emotions, as I continue to walk toward wholeness.

Healing, for me, is not a moment of arrival but a continual unfolding. It is the courageous choice to turn toward what once seemed unbearable and meet it with love. The ceremony may open the door, but it is in the return through the spiral of integration that we truly reclaim ourselves.

There is a teaching from the ancient Sufi tradition that says: "Overcome any bitterness that you may have because you were not up to the magnitude of the pain that was entrusted to you. Like the mother of the world, who carries the pain of the world in her heart, each one of us is a part of her heart and therefore endowed with that certain measure of cosmic pain."[13]

The understanding that I was entrusted with a certain measure of pain from the sacred mother and that I was also endowed with the capacity to heal that pain, for my own journey but also for the whole, is profoundly moving and inspiring. Feel into this with your whole being. You have been entrusted to heal a certain measure of pain by the sacred mother and endowed with the capacity to do so. You are a part of the spiral of life ever weaving. You

---

13 This is a poem in Tara Brach's book *Radical Acceptance* and I thank her for sharing it there; and I share it with you now because I find it to be so powerful and meaningful.

are an integral participant in the interconnectedness of all things. You are responsible for how you show up for this challenge in your life.

How do we heal our portion of pain? The most important agreement to work with for the intention of healing is that healing happens in increments over time, and we are given opportunities to heal the deeper layers as we are ready and able to do so. Whether we've had a supportive childhood with loving parents or a painful childhood with trauma, we all carry wounds. The wounds of not being seen, heard, allowed to flow. We all have inner children who are hidden within. Until we heal and integrate them, these hidden aspects will continue to create suffering in our lives by keeping us out of touch with our inner wisdom and wholeness, hijacking our experiences. Our racing minds and closed hearts are our protective shields to avoid the pain, not just of abuse and severe trauma but all the ways we were taught to abandon ourselves to belong. Our inner child needs to be seen, heard, held and comforted. Comfort and security that were not available can be offered now from you to your younger self. Early emotions that had to be suppressed can be integrated through baby steps of allowing them without overwhelming.

So how does this happen? How do we make all the guests we've been exploring independently in the ceremony of our life feel welcome? The answer lies in attunement.

Attunement Is Integration

Attunement requires presence, the presence to meet the exact vibrational frequency of what is arising within, without distortion or agenda. As we've explored throughout this book, the inner state of presence is accessed through embodied awareness, grounded in the body and rooted especially in the navel center and the subtle, neutral mind. Attuning to the self has been woven through our journey thus far. Now that we've met the inner guests of the ceremony—our energy systems of navel, mind and emotions—we turn toward the frequency with which they long to be met, which is the resonance of attunement.

Attunement allows the wound seeking attention to be met with empathy rather than sympathy; it does not carry an agenda of fixing or an intention to interpret. Empathy is the capacity to *feel* into the vibration of our wound and meet it in its frequency without trying to change it, solve it, or soothe it. Attunement simply means to hold, to be with, to share in resonance. It is a profound act of presence that says *I see you. I hear you. I feel you. I'm with you.*

When we greet the parts of ourselves that lie beneath the surface with attunement, they begin to alchemize, softening, integrating, and returning to wholeness.

As we've seen, integration is not linear. It spirals, unfolding in layers like the skin of an onion. First, we often encounter our louder parts, like the inner victim archetype, which says, "It's not my fault... I can't do it... You made me feel this way." Attuning to this energy means honoring it, not pushing it away or bypassing it. Once the victim is acknowledged and truly met in its vibration, its charge can be released, and its energy reabsorbed into the flow of the whole being.

But beneath every protective part lies a deeper wound. Often, victimhood is a strategy born of survival, an adaptation to a world where taking responsibility felt unsafe. Underneath that layer, we may find the original fracture: a betrayal of trust, a rupture of safety. As more of this material surfaces over time, self-attunement invites us to meet it all—as we are ready.

Of course, we must meet not only our wounded parts, but our protectors too. Our protectors (defender parts) arise to shield us from pain. They also deserve attunement. I remember working with a client who, after a ceremony, admitted that the medicine had shown him how insecure he felt. Tears welled up, the truth rising to the surface. But moments later, I watched as he took a literal step back, squared his shoulders, and said, "I can't be insecure. I wouldn't be able to do my job." That was his protector speaking. A loyal, efficient shield stepping in to keep the vulnerable truth at bay.

It's easy to judge these protectors, but they've helped us survive. The key is to attune to them too, to meet their frequency first, help them feel safe and heard. Only then can the deeper, more vulnerable layers be revealed and integrated.

Self-attunement demands honesty, humility, and courage. The fragmented parts within us are not broken; they are waiting to be acknowledged and welcomed home. Through this process, we reclaim energy once locked away in hiding. That energy becomes vitality, creativity, love. Alchemy, in this sense, is the reunion of what was once exiled. It is the sacred act of remembering ourselves.

Practicing self-attunement teaches us to attune to others, to nature, to existence. Integration alchemy doesn't just require attunement—it *is* attunement.

To attune to our inner world takes practice. It takes the discipline to pause, breathe, and *listen*. As we've discussed, integration is not a mental process. We are elemental beings. Our task is to harmonize those elements within. Fire brings courage and radiance. Water allows emotion to flow. Air grants clarity and peace. Earth gives us grounding and presence.

Connecting with the navel center activates our inner fire, our commitment, vitality, and resolve. Grounding into our roots allows us to care for ourselves and stay tethered to the earth. And the heart center, our internal water, teaches us that by opening to suppressed pain, we also open to love, gratitude, and joy. With these two in flow within us, we then can connect to our subtle neutral mind, to *meditation as a state of being* rather than something to practice or learn. All of it flows together when we attune to ourselves.

Chakana: Elemental Awareness and the Center Within

As we have explored, one of our biggest barriers to the natural rhythm and grace of attunement is the mind. In the ancient teachings of the Andes, I was very surprised to learn that the mind is not considered to be a separate entity or have a singular direction. There is an understanding that it is a thread woven into a living tapestry of all our elemental energy centers within. I find it fascinating that within the chakana, there is no specific direction or element for mind; instead, its presence is everywhere. The mind is the wind that moves through all things, the fire that can rage unchecked or a glow like a candle lit in reverence, fueling our clarity and natural intrinsic intelligence. The mind can be watery like a flood, a deluge, murky like a dark stagnant pool, or flowing freely and in sync with its natural direction.

To understand the mind from an Andean perspective is to understand relationship. The mind relates not just to thoughts, but to land, spirit, emotion, ancestry. In this way, it mirrors the tattvas of yoga and the elemental view of Tibetan wisdom, where mind can be shaped and balanced by its elemental expressions, in attunement with the whole. As within, so without.

Each of the four elements helps us to understand how the mind is a part of the whole.

- Air (wayra) governs thought, clarity, and connection.
- Water (unu) reflects emotion, intuition, and memory.
- Fire (nina) energizes vision, focus, and will.
- Earth (allpa) grounds the mind in presence, patience, and practicality.

And in the center of the chakana, as we have explored, the neutral space where the elements converge, we find the subtle mind, attuned. This is the space of integration, where thought is an ally, no longer fragmented and coming from our adaptive strategies, but instead in connection to and in sync with the body, the breath, and the present moment. Attunement happens here. Integration does not intend to stop the mind but rather honor its place within the circle. We attune to the mind, and when we do we unwind the threads of our periphery to invite the mind to rest in spaciousness through connection to our sacred center.

Now, I'd like to help you deepen your understanding of the mind and how it can actually support and align with our other energy centers, with two practices of self-inquiry and self-attunement. The first is a practice called The Sacred Pause. You can think of it as a mini journey to self that can be used throughout the day as a self check-in. The second is an intentional self-inquiry session that you can use to explore deeper layers of your integration process.

Before exploring either of these I suggest you practice grounding yourself by using the long slow deep breathing introduced in Chapter Ten, so as to invite connection to the navel and neutral mind energies. These practices are ways to sense and return to energies that are dormant in the body, so it's helpful to begin by creating safety in the body through breath. I also invite you to approach this work with a sense of curiosity and humor. Be curious about what is coming through. Curiosity is a neutral energy and if you approach these exercises with it, you're less likely to get caught in resistance or overwhelm. Humor is important. We need to be able to chuckle at ourselves and our defensive strategies, our inner child's warrior charge, our fear that the sky is falling.

The Sacred Pause

Last year, I read a book by Buddhist teacher and psychologist Tara Brach called *Radical Acceptance*.[14] I loved the book so much that I invited a study group to explore its teachings. In this book Brach offers a map to healing that is deeply profound, not only because of its wisdom but also its accessibility. She starts by describing the trance of unworthiness that we all live with (our core beliefs). In the context of integration, this trance can be understood as that which is longing to be healed or integrated from our plant medicine journey. Brach offers that there are two wings in which the healing of this trance occurs in Buddhist thought: the first wing is seeing clearly, and the second is holding our experience with compassion. She offers a tool that she calls the Sacred Pause, and I share it here as a powerful resource for your integration journey.

This practice builds on the felt sense practice that we explored in Chapter Four and entails inquiry and naming our experience in the moment. To do this, we notice in the moment what is happening for us and pay attention. This is a self-awareness technique that can be done throughout the day. I find it helpful when first exploring this practice to set and commit to a specific time to do it every day, such as in the morning while waiting for the kettle to boil, before leaving for work, before preparing dinner, or just before bed. I love to practice the Sacred Pause throughout the day before any transition—from home to work, from work to home, etc. With our hectic multifaceted lives, pausing at the end of one task before turning to the next can bring so much relief to our beings and nervous systems. The sense that we're rushed, scattered, or unfocused can be alleviated with just a few moments of pause.

Self-Exploration Exercise: Sacred Pause

To practice we simply stop activity for a few minutes and direct our attention inward. I find it helpful to first become aware of what is happening

14 Brach, Tara. *Radical Acceptance: Embracing Your Life with the Heart of a Buddha*. New York: Bantam, 2003.

in my sensory world. Next, we start by scanning the body and noticing what we're feeling, asking what is happening, what wants my attention right now. We can then inquire if there's anything needing attention, anything seeking acceptance within; then by listening inward, we can access in the present moment what we truly need. We want to practice this repeatedly, tuning into our body's immediate feelings and the sensations. and then we intentionally tend to these sensations with genuine interest, care, curiosity, and humor.

If this is difficult at first, we might approach our own beings as we would a troubled friend who needs support. If we can name or note our feelings and sensations with the same kindness and care we would if a friend came to us in need, we then start to become aware of our experience on a more subtle level and move out of our chattering minds. When we can greet what is happening inside, particularly the suppressed parts of ourselves, such as the frightened and vulnerable parts, with acceptance and compassion, we create a gentle opening. In this opening we can say, "I see you, I know you're there," with radical acceptance. This makes it safe for the frightened and vulnerable parts of our beings to let themselves be known and integrated.

In the process of writing this book, I've used this Sacred Pause a lot. If I feel stuck, overwhelmed, or have finished a section and am in transition, I find myself sitting on my front porch often. It's spring here in the mountain canyon where I live, and it's so beautiful. As I sit, I have a choice each time. I can either ruminate over the writing process with thoughts like, *What next? How can I explain this? I don't know what I'm doing....* Or I can consciously choose to pause. I close my eyes and breathe. I hear the sound of the mountain creek flowing cheerfully nearby, the birds singing. I open my eyes and see the lilacs blooming, the hummingbird back from her winter home of Mexico. I attune to my five senses. Then I breathe in and see what needs attention. Is it fear, overwhelm, determination, joy? I breathe into whatever is there and give it presence. Just a few moments and I am back, centered to begin again.

I propose this Sacred Pause as an ongoing self-courtship. Take time to connect within, over and over again, deepening through effort and fluidity. Practice this as you continue your ceremony integration. Gently, with curiosity. What is rising to the surface after your journey? Can you meet whatever is there with the two wings of seeing clearly and holding with compassion?

Inquiry as Medicine

Inquiry itself can be a form of medicine. When we meet our inner experience with curiosity and compassion, we begin to unwind old patterns and discover the wisdom they carry. This gentle turning inward complements the Sacred Pause and deepens integration, allowing the heart to see clearly and soften naturally.

"Being cut off from our own natural self-compassion is one of the greatest impairments we can suffer. Along with our ability to feel our own pain go our best hopes for healing, dignity and love. What seems non-adaptive and self-harming in the present was, at some point in our lives, an adaptation to help us endure what we then had to go through. If people are addicted to self-soothing behaviors, it's only because in their formative years they did not receive the soothing they needed. Such understanding helps delete toxic self-judgment on the past and supports responsibility for the now. Hence the need for compassionate self-inquiry."

—Gabor Maté

Self-Exploration Exercise: Inquiry as Medicine

Set a time of 30 minutes at least and find a quiet place to work. Before beginning, I suggest that you connect with the navel and practice the deep breathing we explored in Chapter Four. The ground of healing is made of safety, attunement, and the abiding presence that allows truth to emerge.; thus, before experimenting further make sure you sense these within your being and in your space. If you don't sense these qualities, spend time exploring what is needed for them to be present for you with curiosity. No need to go further.

Safety is key. Are you in a calm state? Do you feel comfortable in your being right now? Is your nervous system calm enough to proceed? A sense of safety is required to continue. If you feel this energy, next come into presence by reconnecting with your natural breath.

Once you have established a sense of safety, attunement, and presence within, continue.

Start with a question for your inquiry. Your question can be simple and direct, such as "Why are my shoulders so tense?" or "Why am I feeling so lethargic?" Your question can also be more complex, such as "What is that part of me that is seeking to be understood, I feel like I'm missing something..." or "How can I make sense of why the medicine was really working in my throat area during ceremony?"

Listen to the story that is created around that question either internally or by speaking out loud. As the story unfolds, direct attention to the body. What is happening there? Is your neck tightening? Is your stomach sinking? Ask yourself: where do I feel this in my body? Can I describe the sensations there? See if you can stay with the sensations and then ask what feeling is expressed here. Remember, we want to connect to our emotions, which become perceptions if not given space, as we explored in Chapter Fifteen. If possible, allow space to feel the feeling. So instead of the perception, which is the interpretation of the emotion, such as "I feel helpless," we try to go beyond that to the emotion itself, "I feel sad."

Now if your sense of safety and attunement continues and you feel curiosity, you can take it one step further. Ask the place in your body you are exploring how far back this feeling goes in your life. Here, we are trying to get to the older, original wounding that underlies the current pain. If we can heal by going back to the place where we were initially hurt, we can heal that wound and all the layers that have accumulated because of it. Remember, in connecting to our navel center we want to be responsive instead of reactive. If reactivity arises, return to deep breathing and let go of the exploration for now. Big healing happens in tiny increments over time and at its own pace. More important than forcing this self-exploration is finding a sense of presence, feeling our hearts and relaxing our minds as we explore our body's messages for us.

Tending the Wound

What follows is an example of the power of accessing the body's wisdom through inquiry from a client session. While this was a guided session, self-inquiry (without a facilitator) can be a powerful tool for integration as well. I saw this client a week after she'd returned from a powerful ketamine retreat in Costa Rica. At first, she said, she had felt better, lighter even. But as the days passed, old feelings crept, anxiety in her solar plexus and an ache of sadness beneath the surface. She told me, "I don't know what's wrong. I learned so much, but now I feel worse."

This is more common than many people expect. The nervous system expands during ceremony, then contracts as it tries to make meaning of what was touched. The integration window is tender and often raw.

I asked her to bring a question into the space, an intention to explore, not one she needed to answer with her mind, but one we could follow with curiosity. She asked, "Did ketamine-assisted therapy actually make a difference?"

Instead of answering, we turned inward.

I invited her to tune into the place in her body where the anxiety was living most loudly. "My solar plexus," she said. "It feels like a stone there. Like I'm drowning." Gently, I asked if she could stay with that sensation, breathe into it, and remember the earliest time she had felt it.

Her eyes softened. Her breath caught. "I'm six," she whispered. "I'm at school. I'm terrified."

Through the lens of Inquiry as Medicine, we met that six-year-old girl with presence and pacing. I asked questions, not to analyze, but to help her *remember* with the body, not just the mind. After a few moments, she said clearly: "I felt alone. No one was there to help me."

When I asked what emotion was under that sense of aloneness (her perception), she paused and then quietly shared: "Fear. I'm afraid I have to do this whole life alone."

And then something shifted.

I asked her to recall what she had felt in her ketamine journey, what she had touched at the height of the experience.

"Fearlessness," she said, without hesitation.

I invited her to feel that memory not just with her thoughts, but in her body. I asked her to call the felt sense of fearlessness from her experience of it in Costa Rica back to her solar plexus, to the very place where the fear had been lodged. She closed her eyes, placed her hands over her belly and solar plexus, and breathed.

What happened next was quiet and beautiful: tears began to flow, not from pain, but from recognition. The part of her that had felt so alone finally felt held. She wasn't trying to *be fearless*. She was simply remembering that she had touched it before. That it lived in her.

And now, she knew how to return to it.

This is what I love about self-inquiry. It's not about fixing the story or explaining away the pain. It's about slowing down, becoming curious, and turning toward the places we've left behind inside ourselves. It's about giving voice to the frozen parts and then integrating the wisdom we've already touched but haven't yet embodied.

What I witnessed that day wasn't a dramatic breakthrough. It was something quieter, but much more sustainable: a reclaiming of self-trust. A deep knowing that the fear wasn't the truth, just a thread in the larger weave. And now she had a practice to bring herself home, again and again.

The Sacred Pause. Self-inquiry as medicine. These are two techniques that can help to bring your integration journey into the body and create balance in the elemental energy centers within. I also encourage you to consider working with a Somatic Experiencing or Compassionate Inquiry practitioner if you are struggling and feeling stuck or confused, as my client was. Sometimes having a person to support and hold space for us is invaluable. Being seen, heard and held can be profoundly healing in and of itself, because usually that which we are trying to heal was not seen, heard, and held when we most needed it.

Ceremony might have brought feelings, memories, emotions to the surface. What is there? Can you be with them and allow them to flow, release, let go? Our minds are tight because we are protecting ourselves from pain. Constant chatter is a way to avoid the more subtle energies within. We cannot wrestle with our mind's defenses; we have to heal what our minds are defending so that relaxation happens naturally.

Our intention to integrate is an intention to work beneath the surface with our more subtle energies and release what is no longer needed. Our protective shields helped us to survive, but now they stand in the way of our freedom. When we weather the storm by allowing our feelings to be truly experienced in our bodies, we are integrating. This process is an invitation; we can say to ourselves, "let me work with my own energies, let me see my mind, let me consciously relax into the heart center." In so doing we create more depth, more maturity, and alchemize.

Alchemy: The Sacred Art of Integration

"Just as the philosopher's stone, with its wondrous powers, has never been actually produced, so psychic totality will never be reached empirically. Consciousness is too narrow ever to comprehend the full inventory of the soul. We will always have to begin again. The adept in alchemy always knew that it was ultimately a matter of the "res simplex" [the simple thing]. Human beings today will learn, through experience, that the process will not prosper without the greatest possible simplicity. The simple, however, is also the most difficult."

—Carl Jung

Now that we've looked at the relationship between our minds and emotional bodies, let's deepen our exploration by understanding the nature of alchemy. As I said above, attunement is alchemy, and alchemy is the art of transformation. Alchemy, in its ancient origins, was much more than a magician's esoteric experiment of seeking to turn lead into gold. It was a symbolic system for personal transformation. Rooted in ancient wisdom traditions throughout the world, alchemy's true intention was the transmutation of the self: purifying the soul, unifying opposites, and achieving wholeness through inner work (sound familiar?)

The search for the philosopher's stone[15], often misunderstood as a literal object, represented seeking the ultimate state of enlightenment—the gold of inner alchemy. In alchemical tradition, the stone could only be created through subjecting base matter to intense fire, symbolizing the transformation of the self through profound trials. In this way, sacred plant medicines can be seen as a kind of philosopher's stone for the modern seeker, initiating a similar process: we bring hidden material to the surface, apply the fire of visionary experience, and, if the body-as-vessel is prepared, catalyze a deep transformation into greater wholeness.

15 Philosopher's stone: a mythic alchemical substance thought to be capable of turning base metals such as mercury into gold or silver. Alchemists believed that it could be used to make an elixir of life for rejuvenation and immortality.

Indeed, plant medicine journeys often feel like a descent into mystery, where symbols, emotions, and buried truths rise to the surface of our consciousness. But the true transformation begins after the journey, in the days, weeks, and months that follow during integration. This process of integration is not linear; it is layered, cyclical, and deeply personal. As we have explored, it involves our entire multifaceted beings. One ancient map that can guide us through this terrain is the alchemical journey, a symbolic process of transforming base materials into gold, which Carl Jung understood as a metaphor for the individuation and integration of the self.[16]

What I find so compelling about Jung's deep respect for alchemy is that he recognized how the early alchemists never separated spirit from matter, or psyche from body. They understood that transformation was not a purely mental or spiritual endeavor, it was embodied. The gold they sought wasn't just a physical metal, but an inner illumination, a refined state of being that came through engaging with the raw, messy, elemental material of life.

The alchemists worked with metals, plants, liquids, and fire, understanding that these held spirit within them. They were not separate from the divine, but carriers of it. There was no split between the outer world of nature and the inner world of the seeker. Integration, like alchemy, asks us to bring together what has been divided. To let the body teach the mind. To let the heart speak its truth. To stay in relationship with what is real and earthy and imperfect.

Jung saw in alchemy a mirror for the human journey of healing and wholeness. He wrote extensively about it, so much so that entire volumes of his collected works are dedicated to the symbolic and psychological meaning behind the alchemical process. He recognized that the stages of alchemy: *nigredo, albedo, citrinitas, rubedo,* offered a living metaphor for what we go through when we commit to transformation. It is a path with a goal, not random, not endlessly looping, but a spiral toward something deeply meaningful.

This is what he called individuation, the becoming of one's true self through the conscious integration of all that has been exiled or hidden. Alchemy gave him a language for this process. And I believe it gives us one

---

16 Psychology and Alchemy (Collected Works of C.G. Jung) Routledge 1980.

too. We don't have to separate our emotional healing from our spiritual path, or our nervous system from our thinking minds. In fact, we can't. True integration happens when we bring it all—body, mind, emotions—into the vessel of our attunement and let the slow fire of presence do its work.

Our next step in our journey together is to explore integration through Jung's four classical stages of alchemy. Each stage offers insight into the inner transformation catalyzed by sacred plant medicines and provides grounding prompts to help you reflect and integrate meaningfully. Meeting these stages with attunement is the alchemy. This is not something to complete but really the journey of healing that spans eternity. I offer this here as a metaphor to work with to deepen your understanding of your own journey of integration.

The Four Stages of Inner Alchemy

Jung outlined a series of symbolic stages in the alchemy process that mirror the path of deep psychological and spiritual work. These stages can help us understand the terrain we traverse through ceremony, and more importantly, in the often slow, spiraling journey of integration.

The first stage is nigredo, or blackening, a phase of dissolution, shadow, and inner descent. This is the dark night of the soul, where old identities, ego structures, and illusions begin to disintegrate. In this stage, we may be confronted with confusion, grief, fear, or existential unraveling. It's uncomfortable, even terrifying, but essential. Nigredo clears the false so the truth can begin to emerge. Many experience this intensity during ceremonies, and the return from this terrain can be life-altering. To integrate what is revealed here requires tenderness and patience.

Following this is albedo, the whitening, symbolizing purification, illumination, and new awareness. In psychological terms, this is the dawning of insight: when the veils begin to lift, and we start to see patterns clearly. This stage invites emotional honesty and the reclamation of denied parts of self. Here, we begin to integrate opposites, light and dark, conscious and unconscious. Albedo might arise during or after ceremony, often in those moments when clarity softens confusion and inner light breaks through the storm. It too requires space and attention.

The final stages are citrinitas (yellowing) and rubedo (reddening), representing spiritual maturation and embodied wholeness. In citrinitas, we begin to metabolize our insights by translating them into discernment, presence, and deeper clarity of purpose. In rubedo, the work becomes fully embodied. The self is no longer fragmented, but unified. We begin to live our wisdom. In this culmination, the alchemical gold is not a literal treasure, but the radiance of a human being who has faced their depths and returned with truth.

In this light, the integration journey is a sacred alchemical process that transforms the raw material of experience into spiritual gold. Sacred plant medicines can catalyze this unfolding. They often initiate us into a direct encounter with shadow, truth, ecstasy, and insight all in one ceremony. But true alchemy happens after the ceremony ends. It lives in how we sit with what was revealed, how we move with what we feel, and how we embody what we've come to know.

Integration is not about fixing ourselves. It's about remembering who we truly are and burning away what is not us. It is a purification by fire, a sacred flame in which the illusions of self are melted, and our essence is refined.

You may have touched all these stages in a single ceremony or found yourself anchored in one of them. Perhaps you experienced the nigredo as an intense shedding of ancestral, personal, or karmic layers. Maybe albedo appeared as insight and inner light flooding through the cracks. Perhaps citrinitas whispered through moments of stillness or awe, a quiet clarity vibrating in your bones. Or maybe rubedo arrived as a profound sense of peace or completion, a homecoming within.

Plant medicine often accelerates this unfolding, compressing lifetimes of transformation into a single arc. But the work of integration is where that arc becomes embodied. You may now be spiraling through these same stages again and again as life continues to shape you.This is the alchemy of becoming. This is integration as art. This is the real gold where life is the ceremony.

Journal Reflection Prompts: Alchemy Stages

I suggest you work with these prompts over time and not all in one sitting. Explore and allow space as needed.

Nigredo – The Breakdown

Nigredo marks the beginning of transformation. In this stage, we might encounter confusion, grief, or disillusionment. We begin to see old beliefs, identities, and protective patterns as barriers. This understanding, though painful and challenging, is the necessary burning away of what is no longer needed. Explore:

What in my life, identity, or belief system is dissolving or no longer sustainable?

What shadow aspects of myself did the medicine reveal, and how can I meet them with honesty instead of judgment?

How can I stay present with the discomfort of change without rushing to fix or escape it?

Albedo – The Illumination

In Albedo, the light returns. Insights begin to crystallize. This stagc rep resents a purification of perception and a peeling away of illusion. We begin to recognize parts of ourselves that we disowned or misunderstood. The clarity gained here becomes the foundation for integration. Explore:

What truths or realizations emerged from my experience that deeply resonate with me?

How has my perception of myself shifted, even subtly, since the ceremony?

What practices or environments help me access this clarity in my everyday life?

Citrinitas – The Awakening

Citrinitas is the dawn of embodied understanding. This is the intention of the work we are doing in this book. Hopefully, as you have worked through the previous chapters, you might experience a sense of emerging maturity, responsibility, and readiness to live more authentically. Explore:

> What patterns or choices am I being invited to consciously change in my life?
>
> How can I begin to act from the wisdom I received, even in small ways?
>
> What values or truths are becoming central to how I live my life now?

Rubedo – The Embodiment

Rubedo is the culmination of the alchemical process. In terms of our integration journey together, it represents the stage of embodiment, creativity, and wholeness. Here, the ceremony is no longer separate from life but rather woven into it. Integration becomes not a task, but a way of being. You alchemize your inner world, not seeking a result but instead experiencing a deepened presence, attunement, and authenticity. Explore:

> What does integration look like as lived action in my life right now?
>
> If my life is now the ceremony, what rituals, habits, or intentions would help me honor that?
>
> What does wholeness feel like in my body and spirit and how can I return to it when I forget?

This alchemical lens offers a powerful metaphor for your integration journey. This is where we work with our ceremony guests in the circle to balance and harmonize their frequencies. We include all aspects of ourselves: our navel, mind, and emotional energy centers. There should be no rush to fix or understand, but a slow unfolding, an awareness and intention with attunement, a return to self by feeling into and finding the frequency, the vibration of whichever stage you are in at the moment and then meeting it with care. Working with these stages as a metaphor reminds us that healing is cyclical and ever-unfolding, carrying us through many layers of transformation, where each stage that we find ourselves in is itself the destination.

Chapter Seventeen:

Trusting the Inner Voice of Intuition

"The very word intuition has to be understood. You know the word tuition—tuition comes from outside, somebody teaches you, the tutor. Intuition means something that arises within your being; it is your potential, that's why it is called intuition. Wisdom is never borrowed, and that which is borrowed is never wisdom. Unless you have your own wisdom, your own vision, your own clarity, your own eyes to see, you will not be able to understand the mystery of existence."

—Osho

It's important to recognize that integration does not come from figuring our experience out. It rises from within, through the fluid energies that exist in our beings, when we connect with our navel, hearts and neutral minds and experience a subtle, quiet, and deep knowing. This is intuition, the inner compass that speaks from a more connected source. In plant medicine experiences, we often can hear this voice because the usual veils are lifted. Connecting with this voice and making it accessible during integration is an important part of feeling connected and centered. From the place of our intuition, we are able to move more gracefully and intentionally in our lives.

Unlike the periphery of our minds, which seeks answers and is clouded by perceptions and conditionings, intuition is felt. It is the sensation in the gut, the pull in the heart, the whisper that says *yes* or *no* before the mind weighs in. It is not always easy to trust because it is subtle, and we have forgotten how to attune to it. Part of the integration process is learning to reclaim this by remembering how to listen to our own inner wisdom.

The practices that we have been exploring of connecting with ourselves through our bodies, navel, subtle mind, and heart centers is an invitation to ourselves to connect to our deeper knowing. We begin to attune to a quieter, subtler guidance system within. Unlike the mind, intuition speaks in the subtle language of sensation.

In moments of stillness, during ceremony, after ceremony, in nature, or in movement or meditation, we may notice whispers of understanding about ourselves and our lives that feel more like a remembering. This is intuition. It has a distinct resonance from within and is a voice that whispers through the body, not the logical mind. When we listen inwardly and trust what we hear, we begin to move in alignment with our life's deeper currents, both our own internal currents and the currents that we choose to swim in our outer lives.

Anchoring Intuition: The Navel Center and the Neutral Mind

"There is a voice that doesn't use words. Listen"

—Rumi

True intuition arises when we are embodied, and when the mind is relaxed. The connection between the navel center and the neutral, subtle mind—our sacred centers—becomes a powerful foundation for intuitive clarity, especially in the delicate work of integration after sacred plant medicine experiences.

The navel center is the body's root system. It is where our natural intelligent instinct lives, the deep bodily knowing that precedes language or reason. When we are connected to this center, we feel anchored in ourselves, able to discern what is truly right for us rather than what is familiar or externally expected. This connection cannot be forced by effort. It is a steady presence that supports a quiet confidence and helps us trust our own truth.

As we have explored, the neutral, subtle mind is accessed through our connection to the navel center. Remember the navel center is represented by the element of fire, the sun. When we are connected to our navel center it is like the sun is shining and giving warmth and light to our neutral mind. This allows us to witness emotions and thoughts without being overwhelmed, creating space to sense what lies beneath the noise. Intuition often arises in this space, speaking softly and readily perceived by our sacred centers.

When the navel connection is strong and the mind is clear, our experience is unclouded by the periphery mind. We become more attuned to subtle shifts, more sensitive to what resonates with us, and more willing to follow our own inner guide. In the integration process, this balance between embodied presence and spacious awareness helps us translate our sacred medicine journey into real healing, real understanding, real change.

The Third Eye

"Intuition is soul guidance, appearing naturally in man during those instants when his mind is calm... The goal of yoga science is to calm the mind, that without distortion it may hear the infallible counsel of the Inner Voice."

—Paramahansa Yogananda

As you may recall, in the yoga postures we have explored, part of the instruction is the third eye drishti (focus point). With eyes closed, we roll them up as if looking between our two eyebrows. Ancient yogic traditions teach that our intuitive capacity is associated with the *ajna chakra*, or third eye. Located between the eyebrows, it is considered the seat of inner vision, discernment, and higher perception. This is also the physical home of the pineal gland, believed by many spiritual traditions to be the gateway to intuition.

The third eye is said to open when the navel center is online, the mind relaxed, and the heart receptive. Now that you understand what fuels your mind and how to open the heart, it's time to explore one of the direct results of these efforts: intuitive understanding. As we have been exploring, in sacred plant medicine ceremony, when ordinary consciousness expands, people sometimes experience deep understandings about themselves and their lives, perhaps through visions, archetypal imagery, a deep felt sense of clarity. I propose that these experiences are all connected to the mysterious energy we call intuition that resides within each of us. As we work to integrate our experiences, we also want to work to strengthen our intuition so that we can sense and learn to recognize our own internal knowing as a steady presence in our lives that guides us forward toward wholeness. In attuning to and connecting to our intuition we can access a vital energy force that brings coherence between our spirituality and our everyday choices.

I learned about strengthening and connecting to my intuition in my kundalini yoga practice. Before this, intuition had been something that I was aware of that seemed to come and go randomly. After practicing kundalini yoga for a period of time, I started to sense my intuition more regularly. In kundalini yoga, we are taught to focus on the point right between our eyebrows with eyes closed, thereby directing energy flow to the pineal gland. I continue to work with this practice as a tool to ensure that I am consciously directing the energy within me to flow upward, and to invite my intuitive knowing to guide me. Here is a breathwork that supports this.

Breathwork/Asana Practice: 4-Stroke Breath to Awaken Intuition

Return to your quiet place and come into sukasana posture, pelvic floor lifted and then released yet still connected, spine vertical, heart lifted, shoulders, down, and chin slightly tucked. Now bring your hands into prayer pose, at your heart center, and focus your closed eyes at the third eye. Once settled and connected in this way, work with your breath. Inhale in four powerful strokes through your mouth, shaped like an O, and exhale in one powerful stroke through the nose. Practice for 3–11 minutes and then follow with relaxation.

Andean Intuition: Reading the Living Path

When I asked my teacher from the Andes what his thoughts were about intuition, he simply took a stick and drew a figure eight on the earth. I understood. Only later, as we were traveling home after our time together at Lake Titicaca, did he share that the wisdom keepers there also honor this subtle way of knowing, though it uses different language. They refer to intuition as *llamañawi,* or eye of the llama, to describe the intuitive, heart-centered perception cultivated by the Andean wisdom keepers. This is an energy that he described as an ability to read the path of one's life, to feel the presence of ancestors, to hear the messages in water, fire, wind and earth.

What is most touching to me is the image he drew in the dirt, the figure eight or infinity symbol. Intuitive energy is rooted in sacred reciprocity. This understanding of intuition teaches that it arises not from striving for ourselves, but from surrendering to one's place within the whole. In essence, by aligning with nature, we become vessels for the wisdom that moves through all life.

Bridging Traditions

By interweaving these traditional teachings, we create a full circle. We must learn to listen to our own inner wisdom rather than what we have been taught is right or wrong in our exterior worlds, through connection with our bodies and our felt sense of what is true. When we do, we become aligned to the wisdom that is found in all life—the creative force. In integration, this means learning to pause, to sense the energy within, to allow our deeper intelligence to guide our healing.

As we have explored, in ceremony many people feel deeply connected to nature, spirit, and truth: a truth that is not taught, but remembered. Integration invites us to carry that connection forward, to remember that the sacred teacher is not just in the plant, but within us. The more we slow down, listen to the body, and create space for silence, the more we notice that intuitive guidance is always available.

Journal Reflection Prompts: Intuition

Where in my life am I being asked to listen more deeply?

How does my intuition speak to me?

What practices help me tune into this inner knowing?

To live intuitively is to live in alignment with one's essential self. This is integration. It means we stop outsourcing our truth. We pause before saying yes. We listen when the body tightens or expands. We take responsibility for our lives, our choices. Intuition doesn't mean easy solutions, but it offers authenticity. And in integration, authenticity is the alchemy.

One of the greatest gifts of sacred plant medicine is the experience and restoration of inner connection. When we choose to come back to that still, subtle knowing, we are no longer searching for meaning outside ourselves. We become the ceremony. The voice we trust is our own.

Finding Your "True" Purpose and Intuition

"You don't have to find yourself. You just have to let yourself go. The path unfolds when you stop trying to control it and start trusting in the flow of life."

—Michael A. Singer

One pain point for many clients I work with is the sense that they are looking for their true purpose and are struggling to find it. The work that they do in the real world may feel like it no longer aligns with them or doesn't reflect their spiritual journey or heart's longing. They may wrestle with this and seek solutions, asking questions such as: "Should I go back to school? I hate my job, should I leave it? I'd like to help people in my work; how can I become a healer?" I went through this when I first started my plant medicine journey and had a private law practice. I was tired of practicing law and wanted to find something that felt more aligned with my spiritual journey. At that time, I had a small private estate planning practice and so my primary agenda with my clients was to help them preserve and transfer wealth. Looking back, I think I felt trapped in a job that had never really suited me. I went to law school with the intention of becoming an environmental lawyer and then found myself working for Legal Aide representing the indigent for many years, which was satisfying to my inner child's need to right injustice, but extremely stressful. When I switched to estate planning, I felt disconnected to that higher place of being in service to those in need, and to be honest I was a bit bored.

I continued with my plant medicine dietas each year and even rented an apartment in Cusco for a while, exploring Peru and from the Sacred Valley as a sacred pause to my law career. All the while, I kept hoping for an intuitive, creative solution to this dilemma. The question: "What is my true purpose?" became a narrative for my mind to chew on. I was experiencing anxious thoughts such as: *I'm not getting any younger. I better decide what I should do next*. Then one day during my meditation practice, I had a breakthrough. I realized that my true purpose was to show up and do everything with awareness, to be present with each task and bring my total attention and presence to it. I felt relieved and freed of a mind game that had been taunting me. For the next three years or so I approached my law practice with this understanding, and it shifted.

I intentionally treated each client as a sacred connection and brought compassion and care into each interaction to the best of my ability. This completely changed my relationship to my practice, to my years as a lawyer, to an imposter syndrome that lurked beneath my practice unconsciously, all of it. It was so healing. And I was so happy when I had an intuitive understanding come through when this process was complete, that it was time to close my law practice and let go. I remember taking all my suits to the consignment store to sell, feeling quite giddy. The freedom that I felt in closing my practice was directly connected to the freedom I felt in choosing to show up in my law practice as a meditation. I had no idea what I would do after hanging up my shingle; there was a leap of faith, trust, but most importantly an inner knowing—my own inner wisdom guiding me, and it all unfolded perfectly.

"I found myself in the heart of everything. In every breath, I heard my calling."

—Lalla

So, if part of your plant medicine work and integration involves figuring out your next move or what you are meant to do as work in this life, I encourage you to consider that your true purpose is to show up in presence, in attunement, and that the outer frame of your life will shift as you are ready. Consider not clinging to your work identity as who you are, but rather another opportunity to show up in the ceremony of your life.

"The intuitive mind is a sacred gift and the rational mind is a faithful servant. We have created a society that honors the servant and has forgotten the gift."

—Albert Einstein

Chapter Eighteen:

Creativity, Celebration, and Joy as Medicine

Together on this sacred path of plant medicine integration, we've given much attention to understanding how our energy system works and how to work on healing our wounds, facing our shadows, and releasing the weight of the past. These are essential aspects of the journey. But equally vital is the medicine of creativity, of joy, of lightness, of laughter, of celebrating life itself. Integration is not only about processing; it is about allowing our true essence of creativity and joy to return, to expand, and to sustain us.

Creativity as a Living Vibration

Creativity is our natural vibration and unfolds when our life-force energy is moving. As we remove the stuck energy patterns within, we reconnect with our natural rhythm, which mirrors Pachamama, to create and to add to the beauty of life. Creative acts are a form of reciprocity. Creativity is the pulse of nature itself, flowing through every leaf that unfurls, every river that carves a path, every sunrise that colors the sky. When we connect deeply to ourselves and to the natural world, we begin to sense that creativity is not an act, but a state of being. It is the one universal life force expressing itself uniquely through each of us.

My friend and teacher from the Andes once spoke of creativity as humans' singular purpose on this Earth, our most sacred responsibility. He was not referring to becoming a great artist or poet but rather the energetic flow that mirrors Pachamama: who is always creating, always renewing, always breathing new life into every moment.

In the process of integration after sacred plant medicine journeys, this creative energy often begins to flow more freely. As we release old patterns, reconnect with our emotions, and find stillness in the mind, the blocks to expression dissolve. We may suddenly feel drawn to paint, dance, sing, write, or simply move through life in more intentional and inspired ways. Creativity is not only about making art; it's also about how we solve problems, communicate with others, care for our bodies, and imagine new possibilities.

Once I was speaking with an elder wise woman who has been a steward on my Eastern meditation path, and I was asking her about my own journey, mainly where my creativity was, why wasn't I writing or expressing something concrete. She laughed at me in a kind way and gently reminded me that my very life was my creative expression. I was a bit surprised and yet greatly relieved and touched by this wisdom, so I offer it here for you now to consider as a part of your own understanding.

In essence, what she was expressing is that when we are in touch with our inner world, our outer world becomes our canvas. This is the essence of integration: turning our own healing and self-understanding into embodied wisdom and letting that wisdom shape how we live through expression, movement, stillness, presence. Just as Pachamama continually creates and recreates herself, we too are invited to create our path, our vibration, the frequency within which we move. Creativity, then, becomes both a mirror of our healing and a tool for transformation. A way to make visible the invisible, and to share what words cannot express. Our unique creativity is our vital life energy, and it wants to dance with creation. By showing up for ourselves and healing, we remove the barriers that keep us from joining this dance of joy and celebration, thus embodying the ceremony that is this life.

Journal Reflection Prompts: Exploring The Natural Rhythm of Creativity Within

Explore the following questions:

When do I feel most alive, inspired, or in flow? What am I doing in those moments?

What forms of creative expression feel most natural or healing for me right now?

What expression is longing to unfold from within me and how can I allow this expression to take form?

Celebration Is Creative Expression

Celebration is a way of embodying the wholeness we are remembering in medicine ceremonies. Celebration can be the embodiment of gratitude and the living breath of transformation made visible. Just as we sit in ceremony to invite what needs to be released, we must also learn to dance with what is becoming, to welcome celebration as a teacher and a companion.

As I shared in the beginning of this book, we close each ceremony in the Amazonian tradition with the sharing of music, singing together songs that uplift, rattling along, and dancing. True celebration arises within each of us regardless of how arduous our journey, how painful our healing, how deep into our own darkness we traversed. We move into joy and celebration because this is how we honor the work we have done, the blessings received, the gratitude we feel for the opportunity and invitation to be a part of the sacred, here, now.

Joy as an Integrative Force

Joy is our true essence and is just waiting to be recognized and felt. Joy reteaches the nervous system how to operate naturally, reminds the heart of its aliveness, and offers a sense of belonging and connection. When we give ourselves permission to feel joy, we create space for the fullness of our experience. In the Indigenous traditions I am blessed to be a part of ceremony and joy are inseparable. The healing is not complete without the song, the dance, the gratitude, the joy at the end. This is how we close each ceremony.

In integration, joy and celebration might appear in subtle moments such as watching the sunset, laughing with a friend, making something beautiful with our hands. As we explored early in our journey together, these are not distractions from our inner work, but rather they are intrinsic to the work. They help us feel safe and in so doing allow access to the body, reconnecting to this wisdom that is our sacred vessel here now. When we reconnect with our essential selves we find our essence of joy, and from this place we can realize that the true ceremony is our very precious life.

To learn to celebrate is to say yes to life. This can be quiet or loud, internal or shared. A walk in nature, a shared meal, a creative expression, dancing, singing, or even simply breathing deeply with presence can all be sacred acts of celebration that connect us to our essential joy.

Self-Exploration Exercise: Joy and Celebration

Consider creating your own rituals of joy and celebration during integration. Some suggestions to integrate celebration into your life:

Consider adding a joyful element to your altar that will make you smile, such as a daisy or silly picture that reminds you it's not all serious.

Connect to nature by bringing bright flowers home for a vase or in the garden.

Create a playlist of music that uplifts and encourages you to move your body and sing along.

Explore finding a weekly practice of dancing, singing, playing, cooking, or creating. What brings you joy? What feels like celebration in your life?

These practices of inviting and remembering joy and celebration are not luxuries. They are tools to nourish and sustain the journey.

Journal Reflection Prompts: on Joy and Celebration

What brings me joy?

What small celebrations can I create to honor my healing?

How can I bring more lightness into my integration process?

Read the verses from *The Dhammapada*, by the Buddha, below and reflect on what each stanza means to you in your life today.

> *"Live in joy, in love, even among those who hate.*
> *Live in joy, in health, even among the afflicted.*
> *Live in joy, in peace, even among the troubled....*
> *Health, contentment and trust are your greatest possessions,*
> *and freedom your greatest joy.*
> *Look within. Be still.*
> *Free from fear and attachment,*
> *know the sweet joy of the way."*
>
> —The Dhammapada, the Buddha

Chapter Nineteen:

The Totality that is Trust

"Trust is in the totality of the cosmos.... there is only one scripture which is spread all around you – in the trees, in the rivers, in the ocean, in the stars. And you don't have to read it; you have to be just silent, and it starts showering on you all its wisdom, which is eternal."

—Osho

Your life is a sacred ceremony that is flowing onward. The undercurrent that carries you forward is trust. Trust brought you to the sacred medicine, and trust supported you through the ceremony. Your presence was not by chance, and trust is what opened the door for your participation. Trust is an inner journey. Think of it as a verb; it is through our action and movement of energy that trust flows and sustains our journey of integration and life. You can access it inside yourself by connecting to your sacred center. With this connection, you can then ride the current of trust and experience greater freedom in your life.

Trust is The Foundation Beneath Intuition

If intuition is the quiet voice within, then trust is the energetic vibration it emanates from. Without trust, even the clearest inner knowing becomes clouded by doubt. In the integration journey, many understandings can unfold and healing on all levels can happen, but this requires time, patience, and effort. Trust is the bridge between our experience in ceremony and the embodiment of that experience. It allows us to surrender to the unknown and believe that what was shown to us in ceremony has a place in our lives, even if we don't yet understand how.

With trust, we learn that we don't have to know everything to be aligned with ourselves in life. The more we participate in this aligned flow—honoring the wisdom of the body, allowing our feelings, the timing of our journeys, and the intelligence of our own intuition—the more we deepen our trust in the process of our integration into wholeness.

This surrender process is essential because one of the most disorienting aspects of plant medicine journeys is the understanding that often emerges: you are not who you thought you were at all. This can be terrifying and confusing. Remember, integration isn't linear but moves in waves of vibration just like the ceremony itself. You might find that one day you feel clear and inspired, the next dark and unsure. This is the natural rhythm, the polarity we explored which is always fluid like the elements earth, water, fire, air, ether. You might fall back into old patterns and if you do catch yourself, come back. When you do, I can assure you that you will have more awareness, more understanding and more self-compassion as you pick yourself back up. You might forget your intentions for a bit, regress if you will; when you remember and come back to yourself, you can then apply that intention with more depth, more commitment. There will be days when you want to go back to sleep, to forget what you experienced, but that inner part of you knows the way forward. This is trust. Alchemy is a process that requires time, experimentation, patience, and care. The alchemical fire must be tended with care before the elements are transformed. Integration is an ongoing alchemy experiment with self. In your integration process, trust is your bridge to the ceremony that is your life.

> *"When I run after what I think I want,*
> *my days are a furnace of stress and anxiety.*
> *if I sit in my own place of patience,*
> *what I need flows to me, and without pain.*
> *From this I understand that*
> *what I want also wants me,*

is looking for me and attracting me.
There is a great secret here
for anyone who can grasp it."

—Rumi

The Sacred Pace of Trust

When I was twenty-four, I moved into the mountains above Boulder. Newly married, I had adopted a Black Labrador puppy named Yuri. Down the dirt road, a woman lived in a rental cabin with a large, black mixed-breed puppy named Kali. She was the same age as Yuri and often wandered over to our property to visit him. I came to understand that Yuri was her pack mate, and I welcomed her presence.

At the time, we didn't have a fence, and the two of them would roam the mountain neighborhood together. Kali was extremely shy. Even after months of seeing her daily, she wouldn't come near me, not even for a treat.

One day, the woman who owned Kali came to my door. I had only met her once before. She told me she was leaving for India for six months and asked if I would take care of Kali in her absence. I was unsure. Kali wouldn't even let me touch her. The woman explained that Kali wasn't just a dog; she was a Mexican gray wolf hybrid from New Mexico. She said Kali could live outside and just needed food, water, and a safe space. Then she said something that sealed it: if I didn't take Kali, she'd have to euthanize her.

Kali had been coming around for nearly a year by then, and I had grown fond of her quiet, wild presence. I couldn't imagine ending her life. So, of course, I said yes. We had a dog door that led into the garage, so I set up a bed for her there, with her food and water.

After the woman left, Kali stayed with us. By then, animal control had suggested we build a fence, and we enclosed about an acre of mountain land. She remained within its borders most of the time, though I knew full well she could dig out whenever she wanted. Her choice to stay felt like a courtesy, a gesture of loyalty to Yuri, and eventually, to me.

The woman never came back. Kali became part of our family.

For over two years, I fed her, sang to her, howled with her from opposite sides of the deck. We hiked together almost every day, her, Yuri, and I, along secluded mountain trails. Still, she wouldn't let me touch her. She never took food from my hand.

And then one day, everything changed.

I held out a treat and she took it. I reached out my hand and she let me stroke her fur. Just like that, she had decided that I was safe. I was her pack.

From then on, she slept on our bedroom deck. She came in and out of the house freely. She even became affectionate, letting me cuddle her, resting her head on my lap. I was able to put a leash on her and take her to the vet. Though she remained shy around strangers, she opened her world to my family fully. This continued for almost ten years.

When she died, I was devastated. She had become and still is my *daemon*, a soul-companion whose love I had not won, but earned slowly, on her terms.

Kali taught me about trust.

She trusted me when *she* was ready, not when I wanted her to. My desire and well-meaning gestures those first years were irrelevant. She stayed true to her inner knowing. And when she finally welcomed me, it was complete. No hesitation. No half-measures. She chose me fully.

Looking back, I see now that's what trust really is—totality.

Trust doesn't arise from pressure, pleading, or even intention. It comes from within. It blooms only when the conditions are right, when freedom is honored, when no one tries to force it.

To this day, I keep a small photo of Kali on my traveling altar to Peru and on my home altar. She reminds me of the sacredness of trust, first in myself, then in others and in the timing of my process. She reminds me that *real* trust is intrinsic, not imposed. Trust is a state of being.

In the context of sacred plant medicine, encountering this state is everything.

Trusting yourself. Trusting the medicine. Trusting that the healing will unfold when the inner being is ready. Trusting the understanding that no amount of grasping or fixing will rush the organic unfolding. Integration is not something we do to ourselves. Integration is something we become. Integrated.

Kali was never mine. She was her own. And yet she included me in her life. And that, more than anything, taught me what it means to trust and to be trusted.

Trust is the undercurrent that is supporting you now as you seek to integrate your journey. Wherever you are right now in terms of your integration, trust is either holding and supporting you or waiting to be invited in from the wings to do so. The journey does not end when the ceremony closes. One might say that the ceremony is just the prelude to the real work. As hard as you might have worked and as intense as your journey might have been, the integration of it is what allows it to take root in your ordinary life. As we have explored in the previous chapters, integration involves a lot of moving parts that are neither linear nor logical but rather fluid and evolving. This requires trust.

What Is Trust?

Trust is an inner innate quality that we are all born with. As we grow, we are taught to trust outside of ourselves and we lose connection to that sense within, but it is there in your sacred center, your navel and neutral mind. This is another remembrance and act of returning. Doubt is created in our periphery minds when we are taught that our natural energetic flow is not acceptable. We learn to doubt ourselves when our natural, instinctual and innate wisdom is corrected by our caregivers. A child who feels uncomfortable around a certain relative might be chastised for feeling a reticence to engage; a child who wants to climb the tree and is told no, it's too dangerous; a child who is told to eat when not hungry, told not to eat when hungry, to sleep when not tired and wake up when sleepy, learns to doubt their inner being and relinquishes their trust in themselves to outside influences. As we learn to doubt ourselves our inner sense of trust goes quiet, so we need to nurture it by listening.

Your integration requires that you trust that you are exactly where you are doing exactly what you need to do to heal and grow. If you can attune here in the present and work with exactly what is presenting for you that is trust. Keeping it simple and not trying to incorporate the cosmic nature of your journey, but rather chopping wood and carrying water, is trust.

Specifically, it's important to trust in your experience as it unfolded for you in ceremony. Know that it unfolded perfectly with the sacred medicine meeting you where you are and showing you what you needed for your healing and understanding.

Trust Your Unique Timing

Next, trust that everything is unfolding at the right time. Integration has its own rhythm and own vibration. Inner transformation is subtle and not a part of this time dimension. Expecting instant clarity, dramatic change, or rapid healing is not realistic; the medicine shows you the work, but you must do the work yourself, one step at a time. What needs to unfold will do so in its own timing as you are ready. Some parts of your experience will make sense immediately, while other parts may take months or even years for you to fully understand. Integration is a lifetime process. Remember, it took you thousands of lifetimes to arrive at the time and place to experience this sacred medicine, and it's all still unfolding within. Think of trust as an action verb, a courtship. As you continue your integration, trust in your process by allowing space and time for its unfolding without pressure.

Trust That You Can Heal

Trust that you can heal. Sacred plants often reveal buried trauma, suppressed pain, and uncomfortable truths about our lives and how we move in them. You can allow all of these to be a part of your healing journey with trust. Trust that what has been revealed has come into your awareness so that it can be healed. Trust that the unraveling you might be experiencing is a part of your own alchemical transformation.

Accessing your navel and neutral mind is the best way to transform trust from an undercurrent to the river that you are floating on in your life. When we doubt our lives and our experiences, it's like trying to swim upstream. When we trust we can relax, and the current will carry us along. This experience of flow comes from connection to our sacred center, as does trust.

The periphery mind is where doubt resides and thrives. If you had a strong experience, your mind might be kicking in with thoughts such as *Am I broken? Will I ever heal? I feel worse than ever.* Consider spending time with these thoughts as they arise without indulging or buying into them. Self-inquiry accompanied by compassion and acceptance is key. Use the Sacred Pause. Ask yourself what aspects of your periphery are at play here?

Bring awareness to the old patterns of the mind that may be trying to hijack your process. Trust that these too are being made visible to heal or shift. Trusting your emotions is a key as well for integration. Whatever emotions are present, can you be with them and trust that they are not bad or wrong but rather invitations to heal and be more present? Think baby steps. Healing happens in tiny increments. Fluidity. Trusting yourself enough to feel your genuine emotions is like a courtship, a dance.

Both the mind and emotional energy centers are powerful allies that have been adapting over lifetimes with the intention of keeping us safe and the tendencies that manifest were originally developed to avoid suffering. Now these adaptations are like knots that we are trying to unravel, and trust is the process of untying the old knots within. When we see how the arhythmic drum beat that is our mind keeps us away from our natural experience and start to open to another possibility, that is trust. It requires trust to create space to feel and experience our natural emotions. When we start to recognize our triggers and remember where they hide inside, when we see and feel and recognize our inner child's needs, we reweave trust. Inner trust. Self-trust. If we can say, "Thank God I can now see this pattern in me and work to heal it," rather than "Oh this is terrible, why is this happening?" we are in trust.

To experience genuine trust, we must have all three energy centers online and in balance. If our minds are anxious or depressed, if our heart centers are shut down, we can't trust. Trust is a felt experience that arises in presence.

Trust Your Body's Wisdom

During integration the body often becomes a playground for unresolved life experiences and emotions. You might experience tension, unexpected fatigue, restlessness, or waves of anxiety in the body. As we explored in the previous chapters, rather than try to resist or push these sensations away, trust your body's wisdom. See if you can use the felt sense exercise, the Sacred Pause, the self-inquiry, to recognize and give space to what your body is trying to communicate with you. Trust that your body knows how to release painful memories naturally through movement, stillness, breath, tears, and voice. Let your body be your integration partner by trusting it. Trust what it shows you. Your body's memory is never faulty, and it never lies.

Trust The Vibration

Since sacred plant medicine work rewires perceptions, memories, and how we process emotions, echoes of the experience will certainly ripple through your daily life. Rather than compartmentalize or dismiss these echoes, trust them by paying attention. Sacred plant medicines work in mysterious ways. As we have explored, sometimes they speak in metaphors. Sometimes they open old wounds. Sometimes they reconfigure how we experience time, ourselves, and connection. There are no coincidences, so trust what unfolds in your life now as the next steps toward understanding and healing.

Trust Yourself

To trust is to say yes, not because you know the outcome but because you know that resisting has only brought suffering. This trust is a spiritual alchemy as it turns chaos into clarity, pain into wisdom, endings into beginnings, and it begins now in the very place you are. This is the fire that you're walking through in the ceremony of your life, and all of these require one essential understanding. You must trust in yourself and trust that you are capable of healing, transforming, and carrying the wisdom you experienced beyond the extraordinary and into the ordinary, into the ceremony that is your life.

The trust required for integration is in the deeper self you're returning to, not the self you constructed to survive. This is the self that you might have glimpsed in the peak of your plant medicine journey. As you begin to alchemize what was revealed—not perfectly, but authentically, not with control, but with grace—you enter the real ceremony of life.

During one of my dietas long ago, a friend asked our shaman what the word for "to try" was in Quechua. He replied, there was no word for try, that they simply used the word "trust."

Another way to say this is: *we try to be but in trust, we simply are*. It's that simple.

To try is to trust. Allow this simple message to support your intentions and commitments. You are moving inward. It will sometimes be painful as you heal the wounds of your own life and the lives of your ancestors. There will be times of great loneliness as you make your way along your own path and follow your heart. When it's dark and you feel like giving up, remember to trust. Trust yourself. Trust your process.

If you trust yourself, then you trust all. Trust is not a quality that you apply sometimes and not at others. It is an intrinsic part of your being. If you trust yourself truly, then you trust your life and you make decisions about how you relate to others which are based on trusting your inner knowing. You trust nature, existence, the divine, not because you learned about it from someone in your past or from a book, but because you have experienced something within yourself that is connected at your roots.

Trust creates freedom. Freedom comes from trust. If we trust ourselves, we will intuitively know which actions are right for our lives and our journeys.

The Living Energy of Trust Is Reciprocity

As we have explored, in the Andean spiritual tradition, chakana refers to the dynamic flow of energy of the four directions and elements that all things are comprised of, including us. The deeper understanding of how these manifests in terms of integration is in remembering the sacred reciprocity that connects humans, nature, spirit, and cosmos. It is not only the energy that moves through us, but also each of us are a part of the relational force that either sustains harmony or does not. It's important to understand that trust is not passive. It is alive, moving, and when in its natural flow, *reciprocal.*

Circling back to the beginning of our journey together, let's look at trust through the chakana and the four directions and elements. First the South, Earth: the energy of grounded presence, release, and trust in the body. In integration, this is where we shed old skins and root into a new way of being. Next, the West: Water. The direction of emotional transformation teaches us to open and allow the energies of our heart center, our feelings to flow. Our heart centers can only be fully open and lead through trust. Next, the North, Air: working with our minds, bringing awareness to our thoughts and creating separation from them by understanding what fuels them. Next, East, Fire: our navel centers, the realm of courage and commitment, where we experience that transformation manifests through the energy current of trust.

In the middle of the chakana lies the sacred center, the place of synthesis and neutrality. This is the space where all elements and directions converge, offering balance, presence, and the silent wisdom of trust itself. In the center, we are not pulled by polarity but anchored in essence. It is here, in this center, that the deepest trust has always been and always will be. Not in the form of any belief but rather as our own intrinsic knowing.

These directional energies are not just symbolic. They can become lived experiences that serve as guideposts during integration and the ceremony that is our life. As we move through our daily challenges and internal processes, the chakana reminds us that trust is not linear but cyclical, flowing in harmony with nature's rhythms.

Trust and Gratitude are One

Trust opens the heart to gratitude. When we trust that life holds us, even amid uncertainty, we begin to feel our hearts. Gratitude arises not from what we receive, but from the profound awareness that we are always supported. In this way, trust and gratitude form a sacred loop, each nourishing the other, deepening our connection to ourselves and our lives, and thereby anchoring us more fully in the present moment, which is when our lives flow as ceremony. Remember the infinity symbol that my friend drew when I asked him about intuition? Here it is in full form. When in flow, we are intuitive, trusting, and in a state of deep gratitude.

Self-Exploration Exercise: Embodiment and Gratitude

Lie on your back with your palms facing up and practice long deep breathing. Scan your body, starting at the very top of your head and moving down to the tips of your toes. Take your time. Keep your eyes closed and breathe into each area of your body as you visit it with your attunement. Internally thank each part as you breathe into it. Feel thankful for your body, which is so complex, finely tuned and sensitive, working in service to your integration. Breathe awareness and light into your being, one area at a time, with gratitude. When this feels complete ask yourself: where does trust live within me? Find that place and place your hands there and breathe into it. Remember.

Self-Exploration Exercise: Trust and Gratitude Loop

Begin with grounding by sitting comfortably and taking several deep breaths, as we have explored, navel engaged, heart lifted, shoulders relaxed.

Center in the heart by placing one hand over your heart and one on your belly. Close your eyes and bring your awareness to your breath, allowing it to soften and slow.

Recall a time when you surrendered to life, even in uncertainty such as a moment where you were able to let go and something meaningful or beautiful unfolded. Feel into that memory.

Feel gratitude arise from that moment of trust, feel into your heart center, breath into your heart center and allow gratitude to expand there.

Visualize the infinity symbol by imagining trust and gratitude feeding each other in a circular flow like a gentle current moving between your heart and to your navel, as in the infinity symbol. With each breath, feel them reinforcing each other.

When my 14-year-old yellow lab Luke died years ago, I felt his passing with such grief. I cried for three weeks every day, and after the tears would continue to flow whenever I thought of him. As I continued to experience this deep grief, a sense of trust that he was okay and still on his journey became a thread that I could anchor to. Eventually, as I remembered him and how precious he was to me in my life, I felt such gratitude for his presence and support over the years that we were together. When I was able to trust his journey and that our time together was complete the gratitude naturally arose within me.

Journal Reflection Prompts: Trust

Free write in your journal on your relationship with trust.

Ask yourself, how does trust feel in my body?

What emerges when I remember that I am supported?

Where in my life can I practice trusting more fully, and how might gratitude help me anchor that trust?

"Relax into your being, you are cherished by the whole. That's why the whole goes on breathing in you, pulsating in you. Once you start feeling this tremendous respect and love and trust of the whole in you, you will start growing roots into your being. You will trust yourself. ... Only then can you trust the trees and the animals and the stars and the moon. Then one simply lives as trust. It is no longer a question of trusting this or that; one simply trusts. And to trust is simply to be religious."

—Osho

Chapter Twenty:

Love is the Heart of Our Sacred Center

"Love should be like breathing. It should be just a quality in you – wherever you are, with whomsoever you are, or even if you are alone, love goes on overflowing from you. It is not a question of being in love with someone – it is a question of being love. You are love. Love is not dependent on the object but is a radiation of your subjectivity – a radiation of your soul. And the vaster the radiation, the greater is your soul. The wider spread are the wings of your love, the bigger is the sky of your being."

—Osho

There is a steady, unshakable energy force of true self-remembrance within each of us. After the visions fade, after the songs have ended and the ceremony is closed, we are left with the sacred ground of our own lives. And here, in the middle of washing dishes, walking the dog, sharing meals, paying bills, lingering in conversation, holding grief, and laughing until we ache, the deepest truth dawns. Life itself is the real ceremony.

With the presence that is love, every moment has the potential to be sacred, every breath a prayer. The work of integration, of carrying the wisdom of sacred journeys into the body of our lived experience, is the work of inner alchemy, from intention to embodiment, from spirit into form. Love.

Love: from Longing to Freedom

When I was twenty-three, I had just graduated from college and was working as an editor for an aerospace company. My college boyfriend had moved back to Baltimore, breaking my heart, and I felt adrift, alone, lost, and unloved. Most of my friends had moved away. Though I appreciated my job, it was high-pressure, with tight proposal deadlines driven by engineers who didn't quite grasp editorial timelines or nuance.

One of those engineers was seventeen years older than I and was and going through a messy divorce with three young children. He was brilliant and capable. He could fix anything. When my beloved '78 Volvo suddenly died, he offered to rebuild the engine. I watched in awe as he tore into the motor with a joy and confidence that made me feel safe. I was drawn to his competence and steadiness.

Our friendship quickly turned into a romance. Not long after his divorce was finalized, we eloped to Las Vegas. I was twenty-four, suddenly a stepmother to three young children, living in a rambling mountain home with a Labrador, a wolf, and two cats. My Cancerian nature craved home and family, and in many ways, this life satisfied that longing. I loved my husband and the children in the way I was able to at the time. But looking back now, I understand that what I thought was love was, in truth, a transaction.

In exchange for stability and safety, I married a good man, *and* someone emotionally unavailable enough that I never had to face my own emotional wounds. It allowed me to live from the outside in. We had a beautiful life on the surface. I felt accepted, loved. But the ache of childhood, the longing to be seen, mothered, and emotionally held, lived deep in my being. No amount of outer achievement could fill that inner void.

I threw myself into self-improvement and service: therapy, law school, triathlons, marathon training. I became the stepmother I had always wanted to have, leading Girl Scout meetings, cheering at soccer games, and reading bedtime stories. I now recognize that I was competing with the memory of my own stepmother, energetically trying to prove I could do better. In attempting to heal my inner child by mothering others, I was operating from a wound. And wounds can't heal through performance.

By my thirties, through long runs and the stillness of early meditation practice, I began to realize that I didn't have a life of my own. I had built my life around someone else's needs and expectations. I looked successful, but inside, I was unmoored and miserable.

After the youngest child graduated high school, I asked for a divorce. My decision was met with shock. Friends thought I was having a breakdown. My ex-husband's therapist suggested I was bipolar, and he made sure I heard that diagnosis. I was alone, in pain, but determined to come home to myself.

The years that followed were difficult and illuminating. I lived alone. I cried, I wrote, I meditated. I walked into the depths of my own inner world. Slowly, I began to love and accept myself. I peeled back the layers of performance and pain, and something softer, more enduring began to emerge. I no longer needed wine to wind down. I began setting boundaries. I traveled to India. I joined group processes that terrified me. I did the work.

In time, I realized that love is not a transaction. It is not earned by pleasing. Love is a state of being. It is who we are when we're aligned with our own essence.

Around that time, I grew very close to a man in my spiritual community. One day, while on a walk, I stopped suddenly, stomped my foot, and blurted out, "I love you. I'm your girl, whether you like it or not." It surprised even me. He was stunned and speechless.

In that moment, I wanted nothing from him. There was no grasping, no expectation. It was simply truth spoken from a deep inner well. Two years later, he called and said he was ready to meet me there. I said yes without hesitation.

That man is Samir, my beloved and fellow traveler. From the start, we agreed that our relationship would be in service to each other's individual journeys. Not to complete one another, but to support each other in becoming whole.

Soon after we came together, we were introduced to the sacred plant medicine path. In an early ceremony, I received the clear message that I needed to let Samir go, that his love for me might be holding him back. I was confused, but I trusted what I heard.

The next day, sitting on a rock by the river in the jungle, I told him, "I'm setting you free." I cried as I said it. I was letting him go energetically and spiritually. I told him I didn't want to hold back for him; and I didn't need him to hold back for my sake and that we would be okay. This took a tremendous amount of courage; I remember feeling afraid, yet determined and sure at the same time. Remarkably, he then expressed that he'd received an understanding of needing to let go as well in some subtle way the previous night during the same ceremony.

The next night, his ceremony shifted. He realized he had been holding a thread, watching over me, staying attuned to my journey, and that it was preventing him from fully surrendering to his own. By letting go of that tether, he dropped into himself more completely than ever before.

What was astonishing, though, was that I too felt something break open. I realized I had not only set Samir free, but I had liberated myself. I had released the subtle need for love from the outside that had defined so many of my relationships, and most importantly my relationship with myself. I felt, in that moment, true self-love. Since then, mine and Samir's relationship continues to grow and expand in intimacy and depth, appreciation, and connection as we support each other and our individual journeys of healing and awakening. This does not mean that our lives are perfect. We can get on each other's nerves at times, but we also are able to come back and always find humor in these moments. We accept each other and are not trying to fix or change the other. We know that we are here for our own journeys and not to try to fulfill each other,

That is love. Not possession. Not performance. Presence. Freedom.

Let's explore.

The Alchemy of Self

"To love someone else is easy, but to love what you are, the thing that is yourself, is just as if you were embracing a glowing, red-hot iron; it burns into you and that is very painful. Therefore, to love somebody else in the first place is always an escape which we all hope for, and we all enjoy it when we are capable of it. But in the long run, it comes back on us. You cannot stay away from yourself forever. You have to return, have to come to that experiment, to know whether you really can love. That is the question - whether you can love yourself. And that will be the test."

—Carl Jung

Integration is not just a post-ceremony process to be completed; it is a lifetime practice of remembering, a spiritual alchemy in which the fragmented self is called back into wholeness. It's the daily devotion of living what you remembered in the medicine space, not just when it's easy, but especially when it's not. The heartbreak, the shadow, the sense of disconnection, the longing: all of these are crucibles. Within them, the gold of your inner alchemy awaits.

In this ceremony of life, love is the essential essence waiting to be remembered. The medicine may have shown you unity, compassion, ecstasy, or truth. But what remains once the ceremony closes is up to you.

What is love? It is the intention to embrace yourself right now, as you are and wherever you are in your process, rather than trying to become someone else who will be worthy of love. It is the decision to meet every part of yourself with compassion. It is the courage to bring light to your inner child, your pain, your fear, and all the adaptations that block your natural energy from flowing. It is your intention and commitment that in essence says: "I will not abandon myself."

As we have moved through these chapters, my hope is that a new understanding of what love is has arisen within you. This remembrance is not a projection onto our external world or those we love, but rather an embodiment, a full body presence that comes from our navel center, our heart center, and our mind center. This love is an energy within us that supports and nurtures us and connects us to the whole. It is through this wisdom that compassion arises.

When we allow space to feel our own pain and understand its root within us, only then can we have compassion for the pain and suffering of others. When we bring awareness to our own experience we develop true wisdom. Think of this as two wings of one bird: wisdom and compassion. Wisdom and compassion come from being centered and connected. Our wisdom comes from being centered enough within to understand and experience our true selves and all the polarities that make us who we are now. Our true connection comes from an embodied sense of self that accepts and welcomes all the polarities within and allows them to flow with love. When we are centered and connected to our inner worlds in this way, love emanates from us, overflowing naturally without effort.

Compassion Rooted in Self-Love

"Whatsoever you can do with others, you must have done to yourself before because that is the only thing that you can share. You can share only that which you have; you cannot share that which you don't have."

—Osho

True compassion for others begins with a deep and honest relationship with oneself. When we meet our own pain with kindness, when we greet our interior worlds without judgment, we begin to understand the tenderness at the core of every human's experience. Self-love is not indulgence but rather the courageous act of meeting our own inner world with patience, acceptance, and care. Without this foundation, our attempts at compassion can become performative, strained, or rooted in obligation rather than authenticity. True compassion flows from humility. Humility requires that we show up as humble servants to the whole.

In the journey of integration, especially following sacred plant medicine work, we often encounter the parts of ourselves we have rejected or suppressed. These moments invite us to practice self-compassion. As we tend to these wounded aspects within, we cultivate a wellspring of empathy for our own pain that then naturally flows outward. We no longer offer care from a place of depletion or need, but from fullness. In loving ourselves, we recognize the shared human longing to be seen, loved, and safe.

When compassion arises from self-love, it carries a steady, non-reactive quality. It is not dependent on fixing or saving others but rests in the quiet understanding that every soul has its own timing and path. This compassion respects boundaries, honors autonomy, and trusts the innate wisdom in all beings. It says: I see you, I honor your path, I walk beside you, not above you. Self-love is the root system from which true compassion blooms.

So, we practice. We get back in the saddle if we fall off. We carve out time for our inner work. Integration is not about fixing yourself, it's about remembering yourself, coming back to yourself, again and again. In that remembrance, what seems broken, tarnished, and stagnant starts to seem whole, polished and fluid. What was wounded becomes wise. This is the alchemy of love, to embrace every aspect of yourself unconditionally. Every act of compassion toward yourself is a ritual of reweaving. You are reconnecting with the sacred within you. When you do this, an outer ripple effect occurs without effort and that ripple is true, genuine compassion.

I once had a journey of a thousand lifetimes in the maloca. I was so far gone, so beyond my own being, connected to all, and as I started the painful process to come home, back into this body, this life, a question arose within me: *Well, what on earth shall I do now?* The answer that resounded through my whole being was: *Now you can begin with your mop. Start mopping the floors for others less fortunate.*

Reciprocity Is a Natural Result of Self-Compassion

"A human being is a part of the whole, called by us 'Universe'... He experiences himself, his thoughts and feelings as something separated from the rest —a kind of optical delusion of his consciousness. This delusion is a kind of prison for us, restricting us to our personal desires and to affection for a few persons nearest to us. Our task must be to free ourselves from this prison by widening our circle of compassion to embrace all living creatures and the whole of nature... Nobody is able to achieve this completely, but striving for such achievement is, in itself, a part of the liberation and a foundation for inner security."

—Albert Einstein

As we have explored together, in the journey of sacred plant medicine integration, we experience many energies that fuel the body, mind, and emotions. If we follow the path of any of these energies to the end, we find that each of these paths ultimately leads us to love. Love is the essence of our being. Love is the essence of existence. It is at the core of our beings because it is at the core of all beings and all things.

Throughout, we have been exploring the energies of existence as understood by the Indigenous Wisdom Keepers. Let's circle back to those now. In these traditions, love means living in right relationship with the self, others, spirit, and earth. Love manifests in reciprocity. When we embody love, we naturally engage in this dance of giving and receiving. We offer our presence, our compassion, our humble selves, and in return we are nourished and receive all that we need. Love is to return to balance again and again by allowing our natural energies to flow, just as Pachamama's energies flow all around us and within us.

As we have been exploring, the Andean understanding of the sacred Four Directions are more than cardinal points. They are elemental archetypes within us that hold wisdom for living in harmony. Love is at the center, and each direction's path seeks balance to be able to connect here.

South: Earth, teaches us to shed the past with love and walk on the earth with beauty. Here, love is solid. Nourishing, tuning into and tending to ourselves is self-love.

West: Water, shows us how to experience the truth of our experience by feeling. Here, love is fluidity and acceptance. Learning to access, feel and release our stored pain, fear, grief is self-love.

North: Air, here, love is becoming aware of our adaptive periphery minds and moving toward our authentic beings. Learning how our minds work to protect us and coming into presence requires tremendous self-love.

East: Fire, here, love is the energy of our intention, commitment, discipline, intuition, and trust. Connecting with our navel center allows us to access our neutral intuitive minds where we can then experience love as an energy within, our very essence. This is our sacred center, energetically reflected as the power of the sun.

Together, these directions and corresponding elemental energies encompass our path to wholeness, and to holiness. In the center sits you, the witness, the one who is meant to embody it all. To live from the center is the journey, balancing the energies and the wisdom of each direction, naturally rooted in and connected to love.

The Spiral Home

Your entire life in this body and previous lives has been pointing back here. To this moment. To this self. Not the self you tried to become or would like to become, but the one who is here now.

Love is the compass that guides you home to you. Love allows you to heal the pain you've been entrusted to heal with your full capacity. Love is the basket you have been assigned to weave within your being. Love is the long spiral inward to the truth of you. Love is the reminder that you were never separate. And as you live that truth, as you embody that remembrance, you become the medicine. Not in words, not in identity, but in presence, in grace, and in your very way of being simply you.

Explore Active Meditation: Atisha's Heart Meditation

This meditation comes from Atisha, The Thrice Great, who brought Buddhism to Tibet thousands of years ago[17]. It is a beautiful meditation for people who want to transform negative thoughts and emotions and experience the spaciousness and compassion of their heart.

I have practiced this meditation for many years and find it to be an incredible tool for feeling my heart and the power of the love that resides there. In Tibetan traditions it is known as Tonglen mediation and there are many ways to approach it. Atisha left us an incredible gift known as Atisha's Seven Points of Mind Training; Samir and I have worked with these teachings and shared them in non-medicine retreats over the years. The meditation sutra that inspires this is simple (but not easy).

> *"Begin with the development of taking with yourself."*
>
> —Atisha

Many meditation techniques encourage you to breathe out your negativity and to breathe in positivity. This meditation does exactly the opposite; it uses the power and compassion of the heart to transform your own worries, fears, and pains and the suffering and misery of all beings, into compassion

---

17 Osho. *The Book of Wisdom: Discourses on Atisha's Seven Points of Mind Training*. New York: St. Martin's Griffin, 1999.

In this meditation, you allow all the suffering of yourself first, and of all the beings in the world to ride on your incoming breath and reach your heart. In its simplest form, you breathe in the suffering, your own and that of others, imagining it as a heavy, dark, or dense energy. Then you breathe out compassion, relief, and love, often visualized as light, sending it to yourself first and then to all beings.

It's not about taking on suffering to fix it, but rather about transforming it in the heart. This meditation teaches you to stay open in the presence of pain, softening the instinct to avoid or shut down, and cultivating the courage to respond with compassion. Over time, it dissolves the boundary between self and other, deepening empathy and the felt sense of interconnection.

Tonglen Meditation Instructions

The meditation has no fixed format so you can play around with what works for you. I have been using the Osho Heart Meditation music (on streaming platforms), which indicates and energetically supports the stages below. The meditation lasts 50 minutes and has four stages. During the first three stages you may stand, move, sit or lie down; eyes open or closed.

First Stage: Connecting with the heart.

Either sit or stand in a relaxed posture and bring your awareness to your body and breath. Once you feel this connection, gently bring your awareness to your heart center by placing one or both hands there. Gently draw each in-breath into your heart, hold it there for a moment, and then let each out-breath flow outward from your heart.

Second Stage: Taking with yourself.

Start with your own pain, misery, suffering and feel it with as much intensity as possible. Accept the hurt, the wounds, and the painful memories of your whole life into your heart center with acceptance and compassion. Breathe in your misery and absorb it into the heart. Let it be transformed there into compassion. Then breathe out this compassion; pour this compassion back out of your heart into existence. You may express what is happening inside you in sounds, words, gestures and movements, or you may let it happen sitting silently. Experiment with both. Listen to what your body needs.

Third Stage: Extend your awareness to all beings.
Now expand this process. Breathe in all of the misery of all beings, unconditionally. Breathe in the suffering of your friends, your enemies, your loved ones, the poor and exploited, the suffering and pain of all beings into your heart. Accept and welcome it there and watch as it changes into love and compassion. Be total so you absorb all sufferings into your heart. Let it be transformed there into compassion. Then breathe out compassion; pour your true self, your love and compassion into existence.

Fourth Stage: Return to yourself.
Lie down, close your eyes, and rest in silence and stillness. Gently draw your attention away from others, from your own thoughts, and let go. Become the witness.

Once you experience how pain and suffering can be transformed into compassion through breathing it into the heart center, you can apply this method silently whenever people and events around you trigger the process. I have been using this practice for many years now and it is really powerful. Sometimes if I am particularly frustrated with myself or someone else, I pause and breathe that frustration into my heart and hold it there until I can feel it energetically shifting into love. Sometimes I must do this more than once, holding it there again and again until I feel the compassion arising. Be playful. Experiment with this. It's certainly more empowering than just feeling annoyed and moving into the projections of the periphery mind.

"Tonglen is a practice of creating space, ventilating the atmosphere of our lives so that people can breathe freely and relax. Whenever we encounter suffering in any form, the tonglen instruction is to breathe it in with the wish that everyone could be free of pain. Whenever we encounter happiness in any form, ... breathe it out ... with the wish that everyone could feel joy."

—Pema Chödrön

Chapter Twenty One:

The Ceremony Continues Without End

"Balance is the highest peace possible, the peak, the climax, the crescendo, because when two things balance—outer and inner, activity and passivity—suddenly you transcend them both."

—Osho

Can you picture a tight rope walker steadily traversing across the Grand Canyon? How does she stay on the rope? Balance. A balance that is created through movement. The tight rope walker sways back and forth and it's this movement that allows her to center and find balance. Her centering point, her point of balance is fluid, relaxed, swaying side to side. With each step her entire weight is held by the rope, and her internal energetic roots are deeply connected to the rope with each step; but her movement is fluid as if she were skimming the rope like a skipping stone on still water. This inner calibration allows her outer being to traverse the rope as if walking on air.

This is an excellent metaphor for our integration journey. We sway between our inner and outer worlds. We sway between our past patterns and our new understandings of what matters. We sway between what we believe and what we know; we sway between our minds, our emotions, and our wiser selves. If we can allow this fluidity without getting stuck or indulging, we can then stay on the rope. If we allow ourselves to get stuck in any fixed place, or lean a little too far either way, we fall off the rope. But thankfully we are not walking over the Grand Canyon. If we fall off, we can pick ourselves back up and start again. We may be bruised and a little sore, but that's because we are on a journey. Feeling centered and connected allows us to experience authenticity, which is when our outer world and inner worlds are aligned.

As we have explored, integration is not a destination but rather an ever deepening, ever spiraling relationship with our inner beings. After the plant medicine ceremony has ended, the real journey unfolds in our ordinary lives, which I hope you might now realize are quite extraordinary. The ceremony continues with each morning we rise, with each breath we take with presence, each night as we give thanks for another day to learn, grow, connect, and let go.

Integration takes place on all levels. Everything is energy and our *energy needs to move*. We are made of Pachamama's life-force energy and each of us contains not just our own unique incarnation but also the whole of creation.

We've explored the understanding that our human bodies have three main energy centers, and each has a unique function and a unique intelligence. In the simplest terms, the center of our intellect is the mind center. The center of our emotions is the heart center. The center of our innate intelligence and grit is our navel center. To fully integrate our journey, we must become aware and work with all three energetic centers. In doing so our intention is to bring these three centers into a balanced connected energy flow. When these three centers are working together and in balance, we are integrated. To try to integrate your experience with your mind or emotional centers is very difficult because the mind and emotions are always in flux and therefore not reliable. Bringing awareness to the navel allows access to the subtle neutral mind. That is integration.

The grounding practices we've explored, anchoring through practical tasks, breath, postures, movement, and connection to nature, create a foundation from which all else flows. Like the element of Earth, they root us in the now. Fire, centered in the navel, reminds us of our power to transform and act with courage. Water teaches us to feel, to move through grief and joy alike. Air, associated with the mind and vision, invites clarity, spaciousness, and discernment.

"Just as the Buddha touched the earth... when the voice of doubt afflicts us, we touch the ground by arriving, on the spot, in this moment. We touch the ground by directly connecting with the earth, the life of our bodies, our breath and our inner weather. We touch the ground by looking directly into the awareness that is the very source of our life. As we connect with what is right in front of us, we realize the true immensity of who we are."

—Tara Brach

Finally, at the heart of integration lies reciprocity: the Andean principle of *ayni*, of sacred exchange. What we receive from the Earth, from the sacred plantas maestras, the spirit world, from ceremonies, we are also called to give back. Whether through offerings, acts of service, or simply living with presence and gratitude, reciprocity should be a natural extension of our inner work.

"What is the next step, the practical application? I will answer that the vital thing is to consolidate your understanding, to become capable of enjoyment, of living in the present, and of the discipline which this involves. Without this you have nothing to give."

—Alan Watts

To live the ceremony is to walk in harmony with ourselves, to pay attention to and balance the elements within, with others, and with nature. To bring forward the teachings from sacred experiences and embody them in how we speak, listen, create, and relate. It is to remember that integration is not something we complete, but rather a sacred way of being in ceremony with life.

Journal Reflection Prompts: Living the Ceremony

Take time to sit quietly with these prompts. Let them guide you deeper into your own experience as you continue your sacred integration.

Roots and Grounding: Where in my life do I feel most grounded right now? What practices or places help me feel connected to the Earth and my body?

Elemental Wisdom: Which of the elements (Earth, Water, Air, Fire) feels most present in my life currently? Which element do I need to call in more intentionally?

Fire: What does my inner fire ask of me now? What daily activities such as journaling, meditation, breathwork, do I commit to practicing so that my own arani within has the friction needed to light my own divine flame?

Mind: What story from my mind am I ready to let go of? What patterns from my periphery have I become aware of that I can meet and let go of as they arise?

Emotion: What difficult emotion have I recently allowed myself to fully feel? What did it reveal?

Trust: What is my relationship to trusting myself in this moment? How can I invite this to expand and deepen?

Love: Understanding that love is a state of being, what practices do I commit to so that I deepen this vibration internally?

Celebration: How am I celebrating myself and my integration work?

Joy: How can I invite my innate and true joy to flourish in my life?

Vision Forward: What is one small, sacred commitment I can make to honor this journey daily? If my life is the real ceremony, what intention do I want to carry with me?

Let your answers be honest, unfinished, and alive. This is not the end, but a threshold.

> *"Your task is not to seek for love, but merely to seek and find all the barriers within yourself that you have built against it."*
>
> —Rumi

We've covered a lot in this book. The invitation has been to explore your integration with awareness, curiosity, and compassion. Below are key takeaways from the journey we've shared. I hope that they may offer you support as you continue your journey.

Seven Integration Keys:

My Barriers, My Responsibility

Complacency, resistance, and fear are barriers that we ourselves erect to keep ourselves safe and comfortable. Only we can take these barriers down for ourselves and this process requires intention, courage, and discipline.

Agency

You are responsible for your life and the choices that you make. There is no sacred plant medicine or healer who can do the work for you, you must do the work yourself. Plant medicine illuminates your path, but you must walk it yourself.

Healing Through Feeling

The healing happens through the feeling. Meet your emotions and greet them as honored guests. The only way is through.

Nature Is Medicine

Understand that connecting to and being in nature is healing. It is medicine. Spend time in nature. Let it teach you.

Patience

Change is hard, so patience is key. Think one step at a time. Baby steps. There is no right or wrong way for you to be at any given time. No step toward your authentic self is ever wasted or lost.

Acceptance

Accept what arises in your integration process with openness, humility, and compassion by honoring your experience without judgment. Let go of the illusion of being in control. All of the tension within our beings, both internally and externally, is rooted in a lack of acceptance. Whether it's trying to change our physical beings, our emotional beings, our mind's periphery, or our outer circumstances. Accepting reality is the key to releasing these tensions within and coming into connection with our sacred centers.

You Are Whole

Consider that you already are whole. Your integration is a returning home to this, a remembrance. The answers that you seek are not outside of you, they are within you.

Daily Practice: Weaving Integration into Everyday Life

Integration is the quiet, sustained effort of weaving attunement and presence into daily life. One of the most powerful ways to honor the depth of sacred plant medicine work is to create a daily practice that anchors your inner journey in your daily rhythm. Just as the ceremonies are intentional and sacred, so too are the ordinary moments of our day when we anchor ourselves in some form of disciplined, intentional practice.

A daily practice doesn't have to be elaborate. It can be as simple as ten minutes of breathwork, journaling, movement, sitting in silence, walking. What matters is consistency and presence. Through repetition, these small self-remembrance rituals become our most powerful medicine. This helps us navigate the ebbs and flows of life with responsiveness and presence rather than reactivity and unconscious patterns.

This commitment to show up for yourself each day is a profound act of self-love and self-remembering. Over time, it cultivates a sense of inner connection that becomes the foundation of trust, not just in yourself, but in the mystery that is this life. A daily practice becomes the thread that weaves sacred moments into everyday living, making your life the ongoing ceremony.

My daily practice is a combination of yoga, breathwork, and meditation that I like to do in the early morning before my calendar of to-dos interferes. I am fairly consistent but find that if I lose connection to this routine because of external factors, it's hard to get back on track. So, I set my alarm and intention and show up. Some days I find that other matters need attention. I look around my home and realize it needs tending to, so instead of thinking I'll skip my sadhana I reframe it. Cleaning house, vacuuming, dusting, etc., then becomes my yoga and meditation for the day. When I breathe into them, these tasks become easeful. Consistency requires commitment and it also requires being flexible.

Journal Reflection Prompts: Creating a Daily Practice

Explore the following journal prompts to help you find a daily practice that is right for you:

When in my life have I felt most grounded, clear, and connected to myself? What practices, environments, or rhythms supported that feeling?

Which forms of practice, whether movement, stillness, creativity, breath, prayer, draw me in with a sense of curiosity or joy rather than obligation?

What time of day feels most spacious or natural for me to connect inwardly? How might I protect or prioritize that time?

What obstacles, internal or external, might arise in keeping a daily practice, and how could I meet them with compassion rather than judgment?

If I could imagine my ideal daily practice, what would it be? What small steps could I take now to move toward that vision?

Based on the responses to these prompts, if it feels right, see if you can come up with a daily practice that works for you, now. Set a consistent time to show up for yourself and follow through. If you miss a day or two, come back to it or reevaluate and find something that feels more doable. It's not about how hard or refined your practice is because *the truth is that simplicity and consistency are the real keys*.

I am inspired by the Dalai Lama, who rises each morning at 4 a.m. to meditate and pray that all beings may be free of suffering. When I feel tired, lazy, or unmotivated, I remember his example and the devotion it reflects. It reminds me that daily practice is not about how I feel in the moment, but about showing up, again and again, for what matters most.

Integration as Service: Healing for the Whole

At its deepest level, integration is not only a personal journey, it is also an act of collective healing. While the path is an inner journey where we must face and work with our own pain and longing, it inevitably leads us back into relationship with the greater whole. Each understanding we embody, each wound we tend, and each step we take toward wholeness ripples outward into our families, communities, and the world at large.

The true heart of integration is embodied presence. Remembering our sacred centers and moving from here, we embody a way of being that is more compassionate and aligned. In this way, our personal healing becomes medicine for others. When we live from greater integrity, when we communicate with empathy, when we walk with reverence for Mother Earth and for all life, we embody a new possibility for those around us. Integration becomes a form of quiet service, rooted not in performance or reward but in presence, an energy from within that will support those still navigating rough seas.

When we show up for the deep work of healing, we are not healing only for ourselves—we are touching the threads that connect us to our ancestors and to those who will come after us. As shared in some Native American traditions, "When you heal yourself, you heal seven generations back and seven generations forward." [18] Personal integration is not separate from our hope for collective evolution. It becomes a sacred act of service, honoring the past, and planting seeds for a more conscious, interconnected future.

This is the essence of reciprocity—to offer back what we have received. Sacred plant medicines often show us that we are not separate from nature, spirit, or one another. Integration asks us to live this truth, not just in sacred moments but in the everyday. As we heal, we help heal the energetic fields around us. As we awaken, we illuminate the path for others. Ultimately the work is not just for the self, but rather for the whole, from which we are inseparable.

Spiraling back: Your Medicine Bag

I hope that you spiral back through the simple asanas, breathwork, and other methods of turning inward provided here to continue to support your integration. Use these tools. Practice them. Cycle through them. Consider them to be good medicine for your own personal medicine bag. I have also provided a list of further resources related to each chapter in Appendix Two. If any exercise or idea interested you or challenged you, I've provided books and other resources so that you can explore deeper.

In closing, I want to share one last exercise with you. I ask that you picture or draw a straight line across a sheet of paper and label the left edge birth and the right edge death. This reflects your life from birth to death.

---

18 The "seven generations" teaching is rooted in the traditions of the Haudenosaunee (Iroquois) Confederacy and is also found in Mohegan oral teachings. See Oren Lyons, "The Seventh Generation," in *Exiled in the Land of the Free: Democracy, Indian Nations, and the U.S. Constitution*, ed. Oren Lyons and John Mohawk (Santa Fe, NM: Clear Light Publishers, 1992), 174–175; and Melissa Jayne Fawcett, *The Lasting of the Mohegans: Part I, The Story of the Wolf People* (Fresno, CA: The Mohegan Tribe, 1995), 14–15.

Now imagine vertical lines representing the *moments of your life*. Consider the possibility that the length of the horizontal line is not important and is beyond your control. What is important, what you can control, and what you are responsible for is *the height and depth of each moment* in the vertical lines.

The height and depth of each moment depend on you. Every moment can be sacred, meditative, or profound. Taking a bath, washing the dishes, sweeping the floor, eating, going to bed, each act can be meditative. The sacred is everywhere and in all things. In every moment of our daily rhythm this potential exists, because each moment contains the whole of eternity. When we're connected to our sacred center, we can remember this and can live it. Each small act completed from this place within is an opportunity to experience our whole potential. From here we can approach our daily lives with the joy and love that is our birthright. We flow when we approach each small moment from this place of presence. Our daily life's work of chopping wood and carrying water can be a chore or it can be our meditation, our prayer. This is my invitation to you. The realization that the real ceremony is your life, every moment a sacred ritual to be approached with care and devotion. This is the alchemy of integration. When we embody this understanding, we are integrated.

Appendix One:

Preparing the Vessel and Entering Ceremony with Intention

I have learned in the lineages of ayahuasca and huachuma that our relationship and connection with these medicines starts long before the ceremony begins and the medicine is taken. The sacred plant medicines begin to work within us as a part of the invitation itself. Their mysterious vibration is felt as we move through our days, bringing situations, memories, and relationships to the surface that long to be healed. Our awareness of these phenomena varies, but within our preparations for ceremonies we are often able to address them. Our preparation to receive sacred plant medicines begins with our intention, our presence, and our willingness to listen within. Preparation is not only about physical readiness; preparation is about aligning the body, mind, heart, and spirit to receive the mysterious miracle that is the sacred plant medicine. This is a surrender to the unknown and an inner respect and humility as we approach the ceremony we've committed to. When approached in this way, the days or weeks leading up to a ceremony become sacred in themselves, setting the tone for the journey ahead.

Just as a garden must be cleared and nurtured before seeds can be sown, the inner landscape must be made ready to experience, hold, and integrate the teachings of the sacred medicine. Without preparation, the mind can become overwhelmed with fear and self-doubt, and the body may become tense, in kind. Preparation creates safety, trust, and openness. It helps us walk toward the experience with humility rather than agenda and ego, and the subsequent struggle that might ensue during ceremony where we end up fighting the medicine, seeking control or escape. These guidelines are inspired by the preparatory diet to receive ayahuasca but can also be applied to working with other medicines.

Steps to Prepare

1. Set Clear Intentions
   Ask yourself: Why am I called to this experience?
   Think of your intention as an offering. This creates a sense of reciprocity for the experience. Write your intention down. Return to it often. Let it be a living question rather than a fixed agenda.

2. Simplify
   In the days before the ceremony, simplify what you consume, including food, media, and social interactions. Follow the guidelines of any recommended pre-diet, and if there are no recommendations, I suggest that you avoid processed food, alcohol, excessive stimulation, and triggering non supportive social engagement. This is a time for inner quiet and reflection.

3. Ground in the Body and Breath
   Spend time in nature. Practice yoga, breathwork, or gentle movement. Listen to the wisdom of your body and make space for rest. The more embodied you are before ceremony, the more easily you will navigate the experience. During ceremony, if the experience is intense, connecting to and controlling the breath through deep breathing is essential. Practicing conscious breathing in the weeks prior will be helpful and supportive in your ceremony work, like sharpening your knife in the kitchen before cutting up veggies for your soup.

4. Quiet the Mind
   Begin reducing distractions. Practice quiet through stillness, intentional movement, or reflection. Journaling can be a powerful way to track what arises as the ceremony approaches: fears, expectations, dreams, those pre-ceremony existential happenings that seem to be working already before you even enter the stream. Ceremony preparation often stirs what needs healing. Welcome this as part of the process.

5. Prepare Your Space
   If you are not in a traditional ceremonial setting, make sure to take care to prepare your physical environment. Make it clean, calm, and meaningful. Bring in sacred objects, natural elements, or symbols that speak to your heart. Create an intentional and calming space where you feel safe and held before, during, and after your ceremony. If you are traveling elsewhere for this ceremony, it can be nice to clean and tend to your home so that you return to a peaceful space.

Preparing for ceremony is about presence. It's about listening for the quiet voice within and trusting that what is being called forth is ready to be met. The ceremony actually begins when you commit to show up, not only for the experience, but for the healing and self-knowledge that will unfold and the deeper work of integration that will follow.

The more care and reverence you bring to your preparations, the more deeply your journey might unfold. The plants are relational. I have been taught that many sacred plants are quite jealous of the energy field they enter within us, and if it is clouded by energies that they are not in sync with this impacts the depth of their work. When you approach them with respect and humility, as they have been approached by the stewards of their traditions, they feel this energy within you and feel welcomed. Also, when you prepare your vessel, you honor not just the medicine but the sacred within you that you are inviting to realign.

Choosing the Right Container: Safety, Integrity, and Alignment

One of the most important aspects of preparation is choosing the right space and facilitator for your journey. Working with entheogenic medicines should not be a casual or recreational experience; it is a deep encounter with yourself on all levels, including levels that remain hidden deep inside longing for recognition and attention. The setting in which you enter this work profoundly shapes the outcome. Not all facilitators or environments are appropriate, and it is essential to approach this step with discernment.

When I meet with clients who are exploring the possibility of a journey to South America, my motto is to *neither encourage nor discourage them*. If they ask me if I think they are ready for such an experience, I tell them that *this is a question that only they themselves can answer.* While I cannot say whether an individual is ready for such a journey, be it at home or abroad, the following cornerstones can be supportive in their decision-making. So, my reader, I share them with you here.

If you are exploring whether a plant medicine journey is right for you at this time, and testing the waters with a facilitator, begin by asking yourself if you feel safe, seen, and respected by this person or group. Trust your gut. A qualified facilitator will welcome your questions, be transparent about their training and approach, and never pressure or rush your process. They should have experience themselves with the medicine and have had *numerous* journeys over many years. I have seen people who have had one or two experiences rush in to facilitate for others, which I find both scary and inappropriate. In the traditions I am a part of, reaching the role of facilitator takes ten to twenty years of deep work with the medicine, without the agenda of training to be a guide.

I see it as a red flag when someone is openly asking to become or identifies as an ayahuasca facilitator after just a few years or diets. The real healers are those who have worked diligently to heal themselves, and the invitation to guide ceremonies or serve medicine comes from their teacher, who is an elder and wisdom keeper through the medicine when that person is ready. Grasping or serving medicine without this invitation is disrespectful and can be harmful to others, and/or can be downright appropriation. I realize that some medicines such as MDMA or ketamine do not arise from an Indigenous wisdom tradition. However, if you find yourself called to work with psilocybin, ayahuasca, peyote, kambo, or huachuma, among others, know that these medicines hail from deep Indigenous wisdom traditions with specific ceremonial rites.

Whichever medicine you are considering, I share this here so that you can be aware of the importance of vetting your facilitator, making sure they themselves have been in the deep end of the pool.

The threshold question is: Does this person possess a depth of personal experience in the type of ceremony they are offering? Then the question becomes: Does this person have experience holding space for others in this type of ceremony? Have they received training, whether in a traditional lineage or modern therapeutic framework? And, do they prioritize integration and aftercare as much as the ceremony itself?

It is also important to consider the physical environment: Is it clean, calm, and conducive to healing? Will there be support if something challenging arises? Are there clear ethical agreements around consent, confidentiality, and interpersonal boundaries? These factors create the container in which your transformation unfolds. Without integrity in the space, a powerful medicine experience can become confusing, unsafe, or destabilizing.

Finally, ask about community and ongoing support. Integration is not meant to happen in isolation. Does the space provide connection points after the ceremony? Healing happens relationally, and choosing the right people to walk with you is part of honoring the sacredness of this path.

If you have any doubt about the integrity of the container or facilitator, consider waiting until a more aligned opportunity emerges. Saying no to a facilitator or setting that doesn't feel aligned is not a rejection of the medicine itself. It's a commitment to your own well-being and intention.

Ceremony Preparation Checklist: Vetting the Space and Facilitator

Training & Experience

- Has the facilitator been trained in traditional or therapeutic settings that make them "qualified" to hold this space for you?

- Do they have experience guiding others on plant medicine journeys?
- Are they forthcoming about their lineage, background, and approach and how they came to serve the medicine themselves?

Safety & Ethics

- Are there clear safety protocols in place?
- Are you free to ask questions or decline participation without pressure?
- Is the environment physically safe, clean, and well cared for?

Support & Aftercare

- Is there a plan for support during and after the ceremony?
- Are you encouraged to reach out if something arises afterward?

Communication & Clarity

- Are logistics (location, timing, medicine type, dosage, group size) clearly explained?
- Do you feel emotionally safe and respected in your communication with the facilitator?
- Are group agreements or boundaries established ahead of time?

Intuition & Resonance

- Does something in you feel a clear yes to this person or space?
- Do you feel seen and supported?
- If something feels off, are you willing to listen to that inner voice?

Appendix Two:

Further Resources for Self-Exploration

The following selections are a sample of resources mentioned in the chapters of this book for your further self-exploration.

Chapter Two: The Quiet Power of Intention

The memoir that opened my path to plant medicine is a beautiful book on healing on all levels:

Allende, Isabel. *The Sum of Our Days: A Memoir*. Translated by Margaret Sayers Peden. New York: Harper, 2008.

In this intimate and reflective memoir, Allende recounts the emotional and spiritual journey of rebuilding life after loss. Among her personal stories, as I mentioned in this chapter, she shares an account of traveling to Peru to participate in an ayahuasca ceremony, offering insight into how plant medicine became a part of her remembering and connecting to her maternal lineage.

I have worked with archetypes in many group settings over the years and have supported advanced process work where we explored the protective roles and patterns we adopt in order to survive, and how these patterns can lead us to abandon ourselves. I find archetypes to be fascinating indicators of our humanity and the unique challenges that shape us. If you are curious about archetypes, here are a few books that have helped me explore their influence in my inner landscape:

Campbell, Joseph. *The Hero with a Thousand Faces*. Princeton: Princeton University Press, 1949. A foundational work in comparative mythology, Campbell explores the archetypal hero's journey across cultures and time. His theory of the monomyth has deeply influenced psychology, literature, and spiritual development.

Estés, Clarissa Pinkola. *Women Who Run with the Wolves: Myths and Stories of the Wild Woman Archetype*. New York: Ballantine Books, 1992. A poetic and psychologically rich exploration of feminine archetypes, Estés uses myths and stories to help women reconnect with their instinctual and creative nature.

Jung, Carl Gustav. *The Archetypes and the Collective Unconscious*. Translated by R.F.C. Hull. Princeton: Princeton University Press, 1969. In this seminal work, Jung introduces the theory of the collective unconscious and archetypes as universal, inherited symbols that shape human behavior and the psyche.

The Path of Love, mentioned above, is an intensive group process that I have participated in twice and staffed many times. It is an invitation to be held and seen without our masks to instead be in presence with others and find true connection and healing. It takes place around the world and has become a vibrant community of fellow travelers. The first time I participated, more than twenty years ago, changed my life. It was also my first experience of needing to integrate. More information can be found at: www.pathretreats.com.

Chapter Three: Grounding Ourselves After Ceremony

Engaging the body in regular movement is a powerful way to support integration. Movement increases vitality, anchors us in the present moment, and reconnects us to sensation and breath. Many community centers and YMCA's offer accessible and affordable classes that support this kind of embodied awareness.

Yoga is one of the most widely available integrative movement practices. Styles such as Hatha, Vinyasa, Kaiut, and Restorative Yoga offer opportunities to build strength, increase flexibility, regulate the nervous system, and invite stillness. These practices are often guided with conscious breathwork, making them especially helpful for emotional processing and energetic shifts.

Dance-based fitness classes like Zumba or Nia can be joyful and liberating. Moving rhythmically to music in a group setting can elevate mood and help release stored energy in a playful, nonverbal way. For many, dance becomes an expressive outlet and celebration of life.

Tai Chi and Qigong, rooted in Eastern martial and healing traditions, are slow, meditative movement practices that cultivate balance, presence, and internal flow. These practices harmonize energy and are especially beneficial for nervous system regulation and spiritual grounding.

Five Rhythms dance meditations, developed by Gabrielle Roth and now carried forward by many of her students, offer a powerful way to move through emotional states using five energetic rhythms: flowing, staccato, chaos, lyrical, and stillness. These classes are offered globally, sometimes under different names. I especially want to honor my friend Vishuda de Los Santos, who brought this dance around the world before passing from cancer.

Osho's active meditations are potent tools for moving energy and inviting deep presence. Many of these are now available on listening platforms. In this book, I reference Kundalini and Nadabrahma Meditations, but others like Nataraj, Chakra Breathing, Dynamic, Gourishankar, and No Dimensions are also powerful when practiced in full presence.

Choosing a form of movement that feels safe and enjoyable is key. Whether slow and meditative or expressive and vigorous, the goal is embodiment—a return to presence, breath, and flow. These practices help keep energy moving and support us in staying grounded through emotional or spiritual integration.

Breathwork is another essential tool. Conscious breathing can regulate the nervous system, quiet the mind, and reconnect us to life force. One of the most impactful books I've read on the subject is:

Nestor, James. *Breath: The New Science of a Lost Art*. New York: Riverhead Books, 2020. This book explores the role of breath in health, spirituality, and emotional balance. Nestor blends science, history, and personal exploration to demonstrate how ancient breathing techniques can restore nervous system harmony and deepen awareness.

Healing songs and mantras can be powerful allies for integration, helping you find your voice, open the heart, and shift your inner state through vibration and sound. Many can be found on popular streaming platforms. From the Kundalini Yoga tradition, explore mantras such as "Ong Namo, Sat Nam, Akaal, the Mul Mantra, Ra Ma Da Sa." In the Buddhist tradition, you might try "Om Mani Padme Hum" or "Gate Gate Paragate," or "Om Tara Tuttare." From medicine traditions, look for recorded icaros from fellow medicine journey seekers or ceremonial chants that resonate with you. Healing music is widely available and invites us to share our voices and vibration out loud, which is so healing. Let these sounds guide you inward, awaken your voice, and remind you that healing is both personal and collective.

The animal medicine cards referenced in this chapter are a gentle, insightful way to connect with nature and archetypal energies:

Sams, Jamie, and David Carson. *Medicine Cards: The Discovery of Power Through the Ways of Animals*. Illustrated by Angela Werneke. New York: St. Martin's Press, 1988. This oracle deck and guidebook draw on Native American teachings and use animal symbolism for insight and healing. A beautiful tool for self-reflection and ancestral connection.

Chapter Four: Cultivating Connection Through Presence

Gendlin, Eugene T. *Focusing*. New York: Bantam Books, 1981. This book offers a simple, body-based method for listening to the felt sense, an inner awareness that, when attended to fosters self-connection.

Levine, Peter A. *Waking the Tiger: Healing Trauma*. Berkeley, CA: North Atlantic Books, 1997.

As mentioned in this chapter, this book offers a gentle, body-based approach to healing trauma that invites you back into relationship with your own sensations, instincts, and inner rhythms. Through methods such as the tapping or showering technique you learn to listen to the body's messages and create a felt sense of safety. This reconnection to bodily wisdom not only supports the release of stored trauma, but it also fosters a deeper, more trusting relationship with yourself.

Chapter Six: The Nervous System as Sacred Ally

As discussed in this chapter, healing can only happen when our nervous system is regulated. This book helped me understand this and since reading it I have also read several other books on the Polyvagal Theory that have helped me really deepen my understanding of how to work with it for myself and my clients:

Porges, Stephen W. *The Polyvagal Theory: Neurophysiological Foundations of Emotions, Attachment, Communication, and Self-Regulation*. New York: W. W. Norton & Company, 2011.

Chapter Eight: Integration Means Integrity

As mentioned in this chapter, I highly recommend: Ruiz, Don Miguel. *The Four Agreements: A Practical Guide to Personal Freedom*. San Rafael, CA: Amber-Allen Publishing, 1997.

In *The Four Agreements*, Don Miguel Ruiz distills ancient Toltec wisdom into four simple yet profound principles for living with integrity: be impeccable with your word, don't take anything personally, don't make assumptions, and always do your best. These agreements offer a clear, practical framework for aligning actions with values, speaking truthfully, and honoring both self and others. On the integration path, they can serve as daily touchstones to live in greater authenticity, clarity, and self-respect.

Menakem, Resmaa. *My Grandmother's Hands: Racialized Trauma and the Pathway to Mending Our Hearts and Bodies*. Las Vegas, NV: Central Recovery Press, 2017. Although I don't mention this book in this chapter, reading it has helped me understand appropriation and widened my lens in terms of understanding my own alignment with others. It's a beautiful book, written with kindness and grace. This book explores how trauma lives in the body, particularly the intergenerational wounds of racialized trauma, and how healing must include the body as well as the mind. Through somatic practices, reflection, and self-care tools, we are guided to repair and strengthen our integrity, both individually and collectively. For the integration journey, this book offers a pathway to embody justice, compassion, and wholeness in relationship to self, others, and community.

Chapter Eleven: Sacred Fire – Connecting to the Navel Wisdom

In addition to the exercises I share in this chapter, I recommend strengthening the navel center as a vital energetic practice. Here are three approaches I use to reconnect with this power center:

Kundalini Yoga's Nabhi Kriya is a powerful sequence designed to activate and energize the navel. Through a combination of breathwork, movement, and meditation, this kriya clears energetic blocks and enhances vitality, willpower, and emotional balance. It strengthens our inner core, which supports both physical and spiritual integration. Sat Kriya, stretch pose, and many other kriyas also strengthen and help activate the navel center.

If you are curious about Kundalini Yoga, there are many free and accessible classes online. One of my favorite platforms is The Life Force Academy, created by Jai Dev Singh, a teacher I deeply respect. The academy offers a variety of classes and practices that focus on breath, meditation, and yoga for spiritual growth and integration.

Pilates is another practice that builds strength in the core and enhances awareness of the navel region. By focusing on alignment and control, Pilates helps develop stability and presence—both essential for healing and transformation. Consistent pilates practice can help ground emotional energy and increase personal empowerment.

Osho's Dynamic Meditation is a powerfully active meditation that includes several phases: chaotic breathing, catharsis, mantra, stillness, and celebration. In the first stage of chaotic breathing, we force our energy from our mind center down to our heart center with the breath. In the second stage of catharsis, we allow our heart center to express itself in totality. In the third stage, as we jump and chant the "Hoo!" mantra our energy naturally flows downward to our navel area, breaking up stuck energy patterns and awakening dormant energy there. It is widely available on music platforms and in-person around the world. This was the first active meditation that I experienced in my early thirties. Doing twenty-one days of Dynamic literally changed my life because the inner knowing of my navel became a compass that I had to follow, even if it meant starting over completely.

Chapter Twelve: The Mind and Integration – Multifaceted

If you want to dive deeper into understanding the mind, these are some of the most helpful books I've encountered. They've accompanied my studies in trauma, somatic awareness, and the art of inquiry:

Schwartz, Richard C. *No Bad Parts: Healing Trauma and Restoring Wholeness with the Internal Family Systems Model*. Boulder, CO: Sounds True, 2021. This foundational book introduces IFS, a powerful method that views the psyche as made of distinct parts, each holding wisdom and pain. A deeply helpful framework for integration work, especially in understanding inner resistance and healing protectors.

Katie, Byron, and Stephen Mitchell. *Loving What Is: Four Questions That Can Change Your Life*. New York: Harmony Books, 2002. This guide introduces The Work, an inquiry-based method for questioning thoughts and beliefs that create suffering. This practice supports self-awareness and clarity, especially useful for integration.

Brach, Tara. *Radical Compassion: Learning to Love Yourself and Your World with the Practice of RAIN*. New York: Viking, 2019. Tara Brach shares a powerful practice to meet difficult emotions and thoughts with mindfulness and love. The RAIN method—Recognize, Allow, Investigate, Nurture—helps create spaciousness and compassion.

Capacchione, Lucia. *Recovery of Your Inner Child: The Highly Acclaimed Method for Liberating Your Inner Self*. New York: Simon & Schuster, 1991. This book teaches non-dominant handwriting to connect with the inner child and access deep, intuitive truths. It's a gentle yet powerful method for healing early wounds.

Chapter Fifteen: Sacred Waters – Emotional Depth in Integration

These books help illuminate the emotional terrain we navigate during integration. They offer compassionate frameworks for understanding, feeling, and working with emotion:

Brown, Brené. *Atlas of the Heart: Mapping Meaningful Connection and the Language of Human Experience*. New York: Random House, 2021. A beautifully illustrated and engaging guide through 87 emotions and experiences. Offers new language and insights to deepen your understanding of your inner world.

Prechtel, Martín. *The Smell of Rain on Dust: Grief and Praise*. Berkeley, CA: North Atlantic Books, 2015. This soulful book draws from Indigenous wisdom to help us see grief and praise as sacred partners. Prechtel offers profound reflections for those navigating personal and collective sorrow.

These resources have shaped my path and teachings, helping me better understand healing from a mind-body-spirit perspective:

Brach, Tara. *Radical Acceptance: Embracing Your Life with the Heart of a Buddha*. New York: Bantam, 2003. A loving invitation to meet yourself fully. This book blends Buddhist insight with Western psychology and has helped many find inner peace.

Maté, Gabor. *The Myth of Normal: Trauma, Illness, and Healing in a Toxic Culture*. New York: Avery, 2022. Maté outlines how cultural disconnection fuels illness and trauma. A powerful exploration of how we can reconnect to our true selves.

Maté, Gabor. *When the Body Says No: Exploring the Stress-Disease Connection*. Hoboken, NJ: Wiley, 2011. This book illuminates how emotional repression affects the body and offers insight into listening to physical symptoms as part of the healing process.

Siegel, Daniel J. *Mindsight: The New Science of Personal Transformation*. New York: Bantam Books, 2010. A clear explanation of how awareness and the brain intersect, and how mindfulness supports integration and growth.

Levine, Peter A. *Waking the Tiger: Healing Trauma*. Berkeley, CA: North Atlantic Books, 1997. A seminal book on how animals in the wild recover from trauma and how humans can reawaken similar healing instincts.

Levine, Peter A. *In an Unspoken Voice: How the Body Releases Trauma and Restores Goodness*. Berkeley, CA: North Atlantic Books, 2010. Expands on somatic theory, offering deeper insights into trauma, healing, and presence.

van der Kolk, Bessel A. *The Body Keeps the Score: Brain, Mind, and Body in the Healing of Trauma*. New York: Viking, 2014. A powerful guide to the effects of trauma on the body and various healing modalities that restore balance.

Jung, Carl Gustav. *Psychology and Alchemy*. Translated by R. F. C. Hull. Vol. 12 of *The Collected Works of C. G. Jung*, edited by Herbert Read, Michael Fordham, and Gerhard Adler. Princeton, NJ: Princeton University Press, 1968. Jung connects the symbolic stages of alchemy to personal transformation. A rich and academic text for those curious about psychological alchemy and integration.

About the Author

Deva Arani is a writer and healing guide whose work bridges ancient wisdom and modern integration. For over fifteen years, she has supported seekers in weaving the insights of sacred plant medicine into embodied, everyday life. Drawing on her studies with teachers across India and South America, and her background in yoga, breathwork, and somatic healing, she invites a path of transformation grounded in presence, reciprocity, and love. Arani lives in the foothills above Boulder, Colorado, where she continues to write, teach, and walk the living ceremony of integration.

www.devaarani.com